"In this remarkable volume, the contributors demonstrate that advances in both science and the philosophy of science require profound reconsideration of psychoanalytic assumptions. The authors deserve particular praise for their nuanced appreciation for the arguments that would challenge their views."

Mark Finn, *PhD, Teaching and Supervisory Faculty at WCSPP*

"The authors, very well versed in both psychoanalysis and contemporary science, illuminate the parallels between the two, with particular emphasis on shared metaphors. The cross fertilization is made clear by their excellent writing and impressive scholarship."

Irwin Hirsch, *PhD, NYU Postdoctoral Program in Psychoanalysis and Psychotherapy and The William Alanson White Institute*

"This volume makes the urgent plea for psychoanalysis to embrace fresh models and metaphors to remain vital and relevant in the 21st century. By braiding psychoanalysis with contemporary science – quantum physics, chaos theory, epigenetics and neuropsychoanalysis – Turtz and Gargiulo offer us an essential and readily accessible guide that enriches our understanding of both the mind and the human condition."

Janet Zuckerman, *PhD, Faculty and Former Director of WCSPP, Clinical Consultant, NYU Postdoctoral Program*

Enriching Psychoanalysis

This compelling collection illuminates new models and metaphors taken from the contemporary sciences and philosophical thought to revitalize and recontextualize psychoanalysis for the 21st century.

The exploration of quantum mechanics, chaos and complexity theory, epigenetics, and neuropsychoanalysis provides the reader with new layers of meaning and understanding that in turn lead to an enriching of psychoanalytic theory and a deepening of experience in the consulting office. The intersection of psychoanalysis, contemporary sciences, and philosophy leads the reader to new worlds that can transform the lens from which one views the psychoanalytic process.

Written for psychoanalysts and psychotherapists, as well as scholars of psychoanalysis that are interested in the intersection of psychoanalysis, contemporary science, and philosophy, *Enriching Psychoanalysis: Integrating Concepts from Contemporary Science and Philosophy* expands the focus and meaning of current psychoanalytic theory and practice.

John Turtz, PhD, is faculty, supervisor, and co-director of the Psychoanalytic Program at WCSPP, as well as former director of the Couples Therapy Training Program. He is faculty, supervisor, and former co-director at the Manhattan Institute for Psychoanalysis. Dr. Turtz is faculty at the New York Medical College and is in private practice in Larchmont, New York, and Manhattan. In addition, Dr. Turtz serves on the Outreach and Advocacy Committee – a joint project of the Climate Psychiatry Alliance and the Climate Psychology Alliance – North America.

Gerald J. Gargiulo, PhD, is a former president of the NPAP Training Institute, New York City, as well as the International Forum for Psychoanalytic Education (IFPE). He served as associate editor and is now on the editorial board of *The Psychoanalytic Review*; he also serves on the board of *Psychoanalytic Psychology*. He is on the faculty of the NPAP Training Institute as well as The Blanton Peale Institute (NYC). He has authored three professional texts and more than 100 articles. He received the coveted Gradiva Award (2017) for his text *Quantum Psychoanalysis*. He maintains a practice in Stamford, Connecticut.

Philosophy & Psychoanalysis Book Series
Series Editor: Jon Mills

Philosophy & Psychoanalysis is dedicated to current developments and cutting-edge research in the philosophical sciences, phenomenology, hermeneutics, existentialism, logic, semiotics, cultural studies, social criticism, and the humanities that engage and enrich psychoanalytic thought through philosophical rigor. With the philosophical turn in psychoanalysis comes a new era of theoretical research that revisits past paradigms while invigorating new approaches to theoretical, historical, contemporary, and applied psychoanalysis. No subject or discipline is immune from psychoanalytic reflection within a philosophical context including psychology, sociology, anthropology, politics, the arts, religion, science, culture, physics, and the nature of morality. Philosophical approaches to psychoanalysis may stimulate new areas of knowledge that have conceptual and applied value beyond the consulting room reflective of greater society at large. In the spirit of pluralism, *Philosophy & Psychoanalysis* is open to any theoretical school in philosophy and psychoanalysis that offers novel, scholarly, and important insights in the way we come to understand our world.

Titles in this series:

Integration and Difference
Constructing a Mythical Dialectic
Grant Maxwell

Psychoanalysis and the Mind-Body Problem
Edited by Jon Mills

Jung's Alchemical Philosophy
Psyche and the Mercurial Play of Image and Idea
Stanton Marlan

For a full list of titles in this series, please visit www.routledge.com/
Philosophy-and-Psychoanalysis/book-series/PHILPSY

Enriching Psychoanalysis

Integrating Concepts from Contemporary Science and Philosophy

Edited by John Turtz and
Gerald J. Gargiulo

Routledge
Taylor & Francis Group

LONDON AND NEW YORK

Cover image: © Getty Images

First published 2023
by Routledge
4 Park Square, Milton Park, Abingdon, Oxon OX14 4RN

and by Routledge
605 Third Avenue, New York, NY 10158

Routledge is an imprint of the Taylor & Francis Group, an informa business

British Library Cataloguing-in-Publication Data
A catalogue record for this book is available from the British Library

Library of Congress Cataloging-in-Publication Data
Names: Turtz, John, editor. | Gargiulo, Gerald J., editor.
Title: Enriching psychoanalysis: integrating concepts from
   contemporary science and philosophy/edited by John Turtz
   and Gerald J. Gargiulo.
Description: Milton Park, Abingdon, Oxon; New York,
   NY: Routledge, 2023. | Includes bibliographical references
   and index.
Identifiers: LCCN 2022012849 | ISBN 9781032221939 (hardback) |
   ISBN 9781032221922 (paperback) | ISBN 9781003271499
   (ebook)
Subjects: LCSH: Psychoanalysis and philosophy. | Science
   and psychology.
Classification: LCC BF175.4.P45 E57 2023 | DDC 150.19/5—
   dc23/eng/20220321
LC record available at https://lccn.loc.gov/2022012849

ISBN: 978-1-032-22193-9 (hbk)
ISBN: 978-1-032-22192-2 (pbk)
ISBN: 978-1-003-27149-9 (ebk)

DOI: 10.4324/9781003271499

Typeset in Times New Roman
by Apex CoVantage, LLC

To my wife and daughter – Mary DeVivo and Amy Turtz – the loves of my life, who somehow put up with me during this project!

And to Jerry Gargiulo and my Peer Supervision Group – Mark Finn, Aviva Gitlin, and Vera Stein – for all their generous support and encouragement throughout this endeavor.

John Turtz

To my beloved Julia and to the many friends and colleagues who have helped in my bridge building between quantum mechanics and psychoanalytic practice. I am particularly appreciative for the encouragement and support that Drs. Barry Barish, Bonnie Litowitz, and Jon Mills have given.

Gerald J. Gargiulo

Contents

Contributors

Roberto Colangeli, PhD, is Assistant Professor and Assistant Director of Research and Operation at Rutgers, The State University of New Jersey. Dr. Colangeli is co-director of the Clinic at the Manhattan Institute for Psychoanalysis and is in private practice in Jersey City and New York City.

John Dall'Aglio is a PhD student in clinical psychology at Duquesne University. His theoretical and clinical research focuses on Lacanian neuropsychoanalysis. He was the founder and director of the Brown University Psychoanalytic Society, and he is the winner of the 2016 Undergraduate Essay Prize from the American Psychoanalytic Association.

Joseph Dodds, PhD, is a psychoanalyst with the Czech Psychoanalytical Society (IPA), Chartered Psychologist (CPsychol) of the British Psychological Society, psychotherapist (UKCP, CAP), Clinical Fellow of the International Neuropsychoanalysis Society, and senior lecturer in psychology (University of New York in Prague, and the Anglo-American University). He is author of the book *Psychoanalysis and Ecology at the Edge of Chaos: Complexity Theory, Deleuze|Guattari and Psychoanalysis for a Climate in Crisis* (Routledge, 2011) and other papers on psychoanalytic approaches to art, film, neuroscience, society, and climate change.

Introduction

Any human endeavor that is not constantly growing is, in fact, receding. This is just as true for physics, the arts, and medicine as it is for psychoanalysis. It is our belief that models and metaphors stemming from contemporary science can make a significant impact upon the continuing growth and enrichment of psychoanalysis. Historically, many psychoanalysts and training centers narrowed their horizons and limited their dialogue with the other sciences in their concern to develop and practice correct technique, precisely understand Freud's texts, and grasp the full import of what is "unconscious." Fortunately, this trend has significantly lessened. This text stands in that tradition – a broader contact with contemporary scientific findings can only enrich one's understanding of mind and human relationships.

The present text is designed to deepen the dialogue between psychoanalysis and contemporary science, which we believe will enrich psychoanalytic theory and practice. The essays in this collection are meant to demonstrate the value of and need for cross-fertilization with other fields of study in order for psychoanalysis to remain vital as an intellectual discipline and as a clinical praxis.

Psychoanalysis, as with human cognition itself, is structured by metaphor. By metaphor, we do not mean exclusively a figure of speech, but rather a primary route to the experience of meaning. The metaphors of psychoanalysis can either be experienced as discoveries or, more usefully, as creative formulations meant to evoke a more deeply insightful way of understanding human experience. As phenomenology and postmodernist philosophy have demonstrated, human beings are always embedded in context. Psychoanalysts today are just as embedded in context as Freud was. The present text will explore how the current context of certain

DOI: 10.4324/9781003271499-1

disciplines within contemporary science can be of great value to psychoanalysis in offering novel models and metaphors for seeing what occurs between analyst and analysand from different angles and from a potentially more creative lens.

Chapter 1 begins with Gargiulo presenting an overview of the major findings of quantum physics as developed over the past hundred years. Among other discoveries, Gargiulo uses the quantum finding of *probability waves* to explore more creative ways of conceptualizing what the term unconscious can mean and how it is experienced. Within this context, the chapter also presents some of the latest findings in our understanding of memory and how best to use such within a therapeutic context. Additionally, Gargiulo explores how some of the most interesting discoveries of quantum research, such as the phenomena of entanglement, can have a surprising role to play in understanding the dynamics of patient/analyst interaction. Such findings, coming a bit late in the formation and development of psychoanalysis, explain and confirm some of the perspectives which Theodor Reik, so far ahead of his times, promoted. This chapter offers a rationale for why knowledge of some basic quantum findings can be particularly useful for the practitioner.

In Chapter 2, Turtz explores what is termed a quantum sensibility, which includes seeing the observer and observed as inseparable, and moving from a Newtonian paradigm of certainty, objectivity, predictability, determinism, and reductionism to a quantum model based on probability, indeterminacy, randomness, and holism. The convergence of quantum physics with existential concepts is also examined.

Following our explorations of quantum physics and its applicability to psychoanalysis, we transition into the fields of chaos and complexity theory. In Chapter 3, Turtz offers an introduction to the concepts of chaos and complexity theory; that is, this chapter introduces the reader to significant concepts from nonlinear dynamic systems theory, explores their underlying philosophical ramifications, and demonstrates their potential usefulness and value to clinical practice. After giving a brief historical introduction to chaos theory, concepts such as fractals, strange attractors, the butterfly effect, holism, emergence, and self-organization are elucidated, with a focus on how these concepts can enhance the psychoanalytic process.

In Chapter 4, Dodds demonstrates the importance of concepts of complexity theory to group dynamics, social ecology, and ecopsychoanalysis. The crucial role of complexity theory to psychoanalytic theory and practice and to the relatively new field of ecopsychoanalysis is demonstrated and expounded upon. The philosophical ideas of Deleuze and Guattari are elucidated to illustrate the links among what Guattari called the *three ecologies* of mind, society, and nature. The significance of ecopsychoanalysis in dealing with the current climate crisis also points to the importance of taking psychoanalytic ideas, concepts, and values beyond the confines of the consulting room.

Chapter 5 tackles the contemporary science of epigenetics, the study of how genes are read and expressed, dependent upon the critical impact of interactions with the environment. Colangeli comprehensively explores how the psychoanalytic clinical process can influence patients at the level of gene expression and consequently have a significant role in reducing the intergenerational transmission of trauma. His study and mastery of sources provides the reader with an in-depth appreciation of the need to resolve trauma lest its inevitable and ongoing presence continues to shadow both an individual's as well as a society's ongoing development.

Finally, in Chapter 6, Dall'Aglio explores the field of neuropsychoanalysis and the importance of having a dialogue between psychoanalysis and contemporary neuroscience. Although neuropsychoanalysis has been an active contributor to psychoanalysis for many years, Dall'Aglio deepens the understanding of how a neuroscience perspective can aid the analyst in becoming more attuned to issues of the body and to working with the mind as embodied. Dual-aspect monism is contended to be the philosophical basis for neuropsychoanalysis, and the conundrum between materialism and the irreducibility of human nature is expounded upon. Finally, this chapter explores the ever-present mystery of consciousness through the lens of neuropsychoanalysis.

The purpose of this text, as we have stated, is to look to contemporary science for new metaphors and models that can expand and enrich psychoanalytic theory and practice. We hope that the presentation of such models and findings, along with their philosophical underpinnings, will broaden and deepen our understanding of the human condition. Such findings have import for analysts of all orientations. From our perspective, an open dialogue between psychoanalysis and contemporary science can be advantageous and of the utmost value in our ongoing strivings to keep psychoanalysis vital in the 21st century. Truth in science is not a treasure to be found and possessed, but rather a guidepost for further experimentation and exploration. *Truth is descriptive, not prescriptive.* Unfortunately, official psychoanalysis has not always remembered this. Had it remembered this, there might not have been so many divisions and splits within the field – all of which have fostered a defensive rather than open and integrative atmosphere. What science has taught us is that welcoming a finding that demonstrates one might be wrong in one's conclusions is simply an invitation for further exploration. In order to learn, one must accept that no human exploration can ever possess any final truth. Hopefully, the various essays in this volume will foster curiosity and creative reflection as well as encourage interdisciplinary cross-fertilization in our endless search for knowledge – if so, our goals in presenting them will have been met.

Part 1

Quantum Theory and Psychoanalysis

Chapter 1

New Models for Understanding the Clinical Unconscious

A Contribution From Quantum Findings

Gerald J. Gargiulo, PhD[*]

"Imagination is more important than knowledge. Knowledge is limited. Imagination encircles the world."
Albert Einstein (1929), *The Saturday Evening Post*

I will begin by briefly summarizing some of the basic findings of quantum mechanics that are generally known and that can broaden our appreciation of psychoanalytic clinical practice. Physics, as we know, is ultimately the study of what things are and how things work. We are conscious of living in what is called the macro world – the world of our everyday life – the world of concrete objects, the world of time. Newtonian physics explains a great deal of how and why, in our everyday macro world, things work. Quantum mechanics, on the other hand, has uncovered what can be characterized as a deeper world, that is, the micro world; a world which is foundational to our everyday macro world. It is here, in the micro realm, where the paradoxical, awe-inspiring, and mind-numbing presence of subatomic fields and particles are manifested; such realties are the foundation to our macro – our world of concrete objects. The subatomic world of forces and fields is the backdrop for our lived-in experienced macro world. What is important to remember is that when speaking of the micro world we are doing so by way of analogy. All we know of the micro world are the words and concepts we have created to gain some basic understanding of the truly mysterious. In what follows I will highlight the confluence

* I wish to thank Drs. John Turtz, Gary Ahlskog, Christopher Rigling, and Ms. Merle Molofsky for their helpful suggestions.

DOI: 10.4324/9781003271499-3

between psychoanalytic theory – particularly its model of an unconscious – and some of the basic postulates and conclusions of quantum mechanics. Any findings that can broaden our knowledge of the world, and consequently ourselves, can deepen our understanding of what we call mind. In this short communication I am not addressing the question of whether psychoanalysis is an art or a science.[1] Rather, by summarizing some of the most basic conclusions that many quantum physicists have reached, we can, I believe, gain a deeper appreciation of the psychoanalytic process. I will summarize some of those most basic quantum findings as a backdrop for our discussion of mind.

One such conclusion, which is basic to our understanding, is that there cannot be a strict separation between an observer and that which is observed. Observer and observed are inextricably woven. Consequently, there cannot be an observer neutral interaction/observation.[2] By observer, in this context, I generally mean *a person*, although that is not necessarily required. The discovery of what is called probability *waves* is one of the most basic discoveries of the quantum world. Probability waves are a conceptual postulate used for understanding what happens, on the micro level, for any observation to occur. Probability waves address all the possible alternatives that an observation can realize. Such probability waves result, when they collapse, that is, when they are observed, in what we name as sub-atomic particles, for example, a proton. Protons are a prototype of sub-atomic particles; they exist when they are observed, that is, not before and not after they are observed. This is a strange finding for us creatures living in the stable macro world. Protons can be understood, however, *as excitations in an energy field*; one can also say, paradoxically, that protons always exist. (This is one of the many conundrums that the quantum world presents us with – partially explainable by remembering that the micro world is timeless.) For our purposes we might appreciate probability waves as *potentiality without specific determination*, until they collapse – that is, until they are observed. Observation collapses a probability wave into a measurable phenomenon.[3] I think it is helpful, when thinking about these issues, to keep in mind that sub-atomic particles are *temporary* excitations in energy fields. Consequently, what is called a proton exists when it is observed, not before and not after. That is, it should not be conceptualized as an enduring concrete object. However, paradoxically, given the timelessness of the quantum realm, it always exists as well – as Heisenberg reminds us. Heisenberg (1958/1999) was one of the major contributors to quantum theory. His formulation of what has become known as the uncertainty principle is foundational. And what does that mean? What Heisenberg formulated can be expressed by saying, "one can speak of the position and of the velocity of an electron, for example, as in Newtonian mechanics and one can observe and measure these quantities. But one cannot precisely measure both quantities simultaneously with an arbitrarily high accuracy" (p. 42). Simply put, to know the velocity of a particle is not to know its location, and to know its location is not to know its velocity. What is important to remember here can be expressed by saying that the knowledge of location interferes with the knowledge of velocity and vice versa. This uncertainty principle, as Stephen Hawking (2002) notes, "is a fundamental feature of the universe we live in" (p. 147).

In this vein and expanding on this finding it is equally important to note another basic and fundamental finding of quantum research. That is, as Brody (2020) notes, "measurement creates objectively real states." What we experience as reality "does not exist prior to the measurement" (p. 83). Measurement – not a passive measuring but rather some form of interaction – creates what is observed. Such a finding is not an endorsement for capriciousness but an odd fact about the quantum world. The full significance of this finding is hard to grasp in our everyday life experiences. The world we experience is created by our interaction and observation. It is a world of interactive relationships, not a world of permanent objects.[4] What I am proposing is that this conclusion can serve as a helpful analogy for our understanding of mind. I will return to this thought shortly.

As I have noted a proton, for example, can manifest itself either as a wave or as a discrete particle, depending on how an individual quantum observation is structured. This is a remarkable finding. What at first sight might seem rather arbitrary is, in fact, revelatory. Likewise, and only by way of analogy, we can note that the apparently individual, somewhat idiosyncratic nature of psychoanalytic practice does not disqualify it for objective study.

In the sub-atomic realm, *probability waves* are everywhere and nowhere until they collapse; collapse, in this context, meaning they are experienced as an observable reality. As a layman in physics, I think of probability waves as *the possibility of going from the generically possible to the measurable actual*. The quantum world is unknowable in itself; we create models to try to explain some of its most basic findings. All we know of the quantum world is the language we have used to try to describe it. That is, for example, the sub-atomic level can be understood as a world of proba-bility waves. We might speak of such a world as *open-ended*. We can build a bridge here with clinical experience, I believe, by noting that an analyst brings a similar open-ended possibility to the naming of what a patient is experiencing and, in the naming, concretizes – that is, creates – what was, before the naming, just open-ended possibilities.

Another important finding is that the micro world operates within a framework of high probability rather than strict determinism. Conse-quently, any strict deterministic model, be it neurological, philosophi-cal, or psychoanalytic, betrays a basic misunderstanding of what we now understand of reality at its most foundational level. Rovelli (2018) clari-fies this by noting that " 'Fluctuation' does not mean that what happens is never determined. It means that it is determined only at certain moments, and in an unpredictable way. Indeterminacy is resolved when a quantity interacts with something else."[5] Strict determinism informed the scientific community for hundreds of years, but when the evidence suggested oth-erwise, the scientific community followed. Such a willingness to change a most basic assumption shows the difference between an ideology and a science.[6,7] Science is marked by a continuous testing and verification of its models and findings as well as a willingness to learn from whatever errors occur.[8]

Macro Models

Freud conceptualized his major findings prior to the discoveries of quan-tum mechanics circa 1925. He employed Newtonian models as a frame-work for many of his conclusions. Psychoanalytic clinical practice, as we know, assumed that it was possible for an analyst to be personally involved but simultaneously to be a relatively neutral participant as well. Within such a context, Freud's (2005) reliance on determinism as one of the pil-lars of *free association* (notwithstanding multi-determination) was simply assumed.[9] Functioning within such a framework, the inevitable possibil-ity of close to exact discoverability, given careful analysis, particularly as reflected in *The Psychopathology of Everyday Life* (Freud, 1965a), was a therapeutic goal in theory if not always in practice. (Free association, as we know, implies that a patient, as one of the end goals of treatment, can speak freely and openly about anything she or he might be thinking or musing about.)

What quantum findings have established is that *strict determinism* can no longer be assumed. Despite Einstein's belief, God does, in fact, *play dice* with the world. Extending a quantum model framework to our experiences of mind, we can say that human beings also play dice with their associations, their memories, and their imagination. Instead of strict determinism, quantum findings suggest a high probability model that reflects more accurately what human beings experience in their thinking and phantasizing. Such a framework both deepens and grounds *surprise* for both participants in therapy (see Reik, 1936). Put another way, we can say that a patient is more free than classical psychoanalysis has assumed. Using a quantum model of the collapse of a probability wave guarantees, *by way of analogy*, the possibility of appreciating free associations on a deeper level.

As we know, how an analyst interacts with a patient is contributory to what such a patient remembers. That is what John Wheeler, of Princeton University, meant by his seemingly obvious statement that *the questions we ask determine the answers we get.* (We create the world we live in by the questions we ask.) All that one can expect in listening to a patient's associations, for example, is to understand that such associations reflect a high probability of what a patient *might* be experiencing at that moment. One informative conclusion from such a finding is to recognize that what is *created* by interpretation/interaction is what is simultaneously uncovered. That is, discoveries in therapy are more of a new creation rather than a remembrance from the past. Kumar (2008) is particularly helpful here: "A particle's momentum becomes 'real' only when it interacts with a device designed to measure its momentum" (p. 311). That is, a particle is there waiting (by means of a probability wave) to be created, so to speak, analogous to what a patient brings to therapy – but which is only created by interaction, that is by interpretation. We can extend this finding and speak to the issue of memory. Memory, as we know, is not a digital reproduction. That is, each memory is a new edition and consequently a new creation.[10]

The point of interest for us at this juncture is to conclude, if we follow what is known as the Copenhagen interpretation of quantum findings, that observation, that is, measurement, creates the foundations of our experienced world. We are obviously not aware of this in our everyday experiences. In our everyday world physicists posit what is called *decoherence* to explain how everything we experience is a measured interaction with everything else. I will be using such a conclusion, along with the finding of high probability, *by way of analogy*, to broaden our understanding of the clinical unconscious.

The Clinical Unconscious[11]

For all of Freud's desires to make psychoanalysis a scientific enterprise, we are, ultimately, negotiating with Freud's intellectual constructs and models, reflecting not only his clinical studies but also his creative imagination. Freud alludes to this himself when he speaks about his myths and his case studies – which, he states, read more like novellas. Such an observation applies as well to one of his most basic postulates; that is, his explanatory model of a clinical unconscious. All too often one forgets that such a concept, as Freud himself notes, is a postulate; a postulate to explain certain phenomena. Consequently, such a hypothesis, such an unconscious should not, I believe, be spoken of as if it were a noun. (Notwithstanding the grammatical difficulties with the words "the" or "an.") Such a postulate is better appreciated as a construct, a model, to help explain phenomena that are otherwise not as easily explainable. Unfortunately, in his seminal work *On the Unconscious*, Freud (2005) initially sidesteps the notion of a postulate and speaks of such an unconscious as an "existing living thing . . . capable of development" (p. 73). Freud goes on to say that what is in such an unconscious is *immortal and timeless* (p. 69). Such statements are dramatic and engaging, but difficult to justify. There is no time in the micro world since the micro world is non-entropic, and there is nothing immortal in our macro world either. Entropy, as we know, means things fall apart and become disorganized. There is nothing immortal in our macro world since it is a world of progressive disorganization – a world where entropy holds sway. Given his assumptions, Freud could justifiably speak of himself as a discoverer of a new land, which in a real sense he was – but in many respects it was a land that he created. He was, however, mistaken to think that prior to his discoveries consciousness was valued more than what we name as unconscious. Dehaene has clarified this when he notes "Centuries before Freud, many philosophers – including Saint Augustine, Thomas Aquinas, Descartes, Spinoza and Leibniz noted that the course of human action is driven by a broad array of mechanisms that are inaccessible to introspection, from sensorimotor reflexes to unaware motives and hidden desires" (p. 51).[12]

What I am addressing in these reflections is the understanding that such an unconscious should not be conceptualized as a noun. It is not, in itself, an *existing living thing* (p. 73).[13] That most of our biological, neurological as well as intellectual functions are non-conscious is an obvious given; consequently, "unconscious" is best understood as a descriptive adjective. What we experience as consciousness is a result of the brain's unconscious functions. Addressing consciousness, Dehaene (2014) notes: "The proposal is simple: consciousness is brain-wide information sharing" (p. 161). The question is far from settled; new theories continue to deepen our understanding. Solms (2021) approaches the topic with a very sophisticated discussion of consciousness when he notes, "consciousness at its source is affect. Then it is extended outwards onto perception, to evaluate perceptual inferences" (p. 189).[14] Consciousness, as we know, is particularly difficult to understand.

Just as the micro world is made meaningful by some form of interactive experience (observation/measurement), so likewise is the *repressed unconscious* actualized by interpretative interaction. This is similar to how a proton is actualized by observation. That is, interpretation, in clinical experience, serves the same end. Just as energy fields and probability waves are basic for understanding for what we name as the micro world, so likewise are probability waves a *helpful analogy*, I believe, for understanding what is understood as unconscious, particularly the repressed unconscious.[15] We are talking about process over content, of interaction over separateness. Rovelli (2018) addresses such a perspective when he notes: "We can think of the world as made up of things. Of substances. Of entities. Of something that is. Or we can think of it as made up of events. Of happenings. Of processes. Of something that occurs" (p. 97). Quantum findings support our understanding the world as *something that occurs*. Employing such a model, repression, for example, is, as we know, something that is ongoing.

To summarize, *probability waves* refer to a range of possibilities for the *probable location* of a proton; it is one of the core models of quantum mechanics. Just as an observation collapses a probability wave, thereby making possible the observation of a sub-atomic presence (object), so likewise, as mentioned, the clinical repressed unconscious comes to be through an analyst's interpretation. *I am comparing the notion of an ongoing unconscious here to the range of probability waves quantum mechanics posits.* The Copenhagen interpretation of quantum mechanics maintains that *reality does not exist until it is measured* – meaning observed/measured. I am making the same postulate for what we name as the repressed unconscious. Dehaene (2014) speaks to this when he notes, "Many experiments show that subliminal stimuli undergo a rapid exponential decay in the brain. Summarizing these findings, my colleague Lionel Naccache concluded . . . that 'The unconscious is not structured as a language but as a decaying exponential.'. . . Only consciousness allows us to entertain lasting thoughts" (p. 104).

As mentioned, the unconscious is not, despite Freud's language, a "living thing in itself." In classical Freudian thought it cannot be known, just as the micro world is not known in itself; what is known are our mental descriptions of it – echoing Niels Bohr's observations. The repressed unconscious is a descriptive model of a dynamic process and should not be categorized as a noun.[16] Consequently, analysts are not archeologists, as per Freud's metaphor, but rather creative observers/contributors. Theodor Reik's writings highlight the cultural dimensions of such clinical experience.

As mentioned, the clinical unconscious is not a noun; the term refers to a psychological construct, that is, an intellectual model. It is not a concrete thing. One might say it is as elusive as a proton. It is knowable when it is interpreted. Perhaps the repressed unconscious might be better understood as a metaphor to describe certain non-conscious information that is the consequence of psychological defenses.

A proton can be understood as an excitation in an energy field.[17] Likewise, the repressed unconscious has no dimensions, it can be spoken of as a world of high probabilities – just as the micro world is a world of high probabilities. It is actualized out of a myriad of possibilities that are realized by what the analyst and/or patient bring to their encounter.[18] The descriptive unconscious, as we know, means that a major portion of what we call mind is non-conscious. The repressed unconscious means that human beings can never have complete awareness of the psychological realities influencing their thoughts and behavior.[19] In a previous publication (2016), I noted:

Lifting repression is identifying a phenomenon as repressed. But if this is the case, what are we to make of Freud's theory of a counterforce keeping such phenomena out of consciousness? Obviously, there is no single counterforce but rather an array of defenses, the psychoanalytic metaphors, which explain the various personal and sometimes communal strategies used to not recognize, or accept, or explain, behavior or beliefs, all of which serve the purpose of unawareness. Such an approach makes more sense of Freud's cryptic remark that at the end of analysis a patient usually affirms that he or she knew it all along.

(p. 27)

To split off, to deny, to isolate a thought, memory, or feeling does not mean they are put *someplace* in the mind.

In summary, we can note that either the patient and/or the analyst actualizes, that is, creates the clinical/repressed unconscious by her or his selection (interactive/observation) of material to respond to, observe, or interpret.[20] Freud speaks about his unconscious as timeless, but a "timeless unconscious" is problematic; the experience of, or the living out of, or the eventual awareness of a repressed phantasy always occurs within the time dimensions of an individual living in the macro world. That human beings can be influenced by non-conscious thoughts/phantasies was not first discovered by Freud; his insight was in showing how such non-conscious realities (and defenses) influence behavior. Additionally, his developing a technique to address, explore, and resolve such defenses was a second moment of his genius.

What a clinical psychoanalytic interpretation implies is both varied and open-ended, similar to the measuring results in quantum physics. When making an interpretation addressing a patient's past, an analyst is not primarily excavating and preserving something from the past. Rather, both analyst and patient are (re)creating the past in the present. But it is a past waiting, so to speak, to be created. That is what I mean by everything, is in the now. All we have is the present.

To repeat, interpretations of what we call unconscious material are creative participant/observer creations, not acts of excavations. The past is constantly being recreated and consequently re-experienced – as *a new edition* – depending on who and where we are and what is going on in the present.

Perhaps an unconscious, along with pre-consciousness and consciousness, might better be spoken of as psychic dimensions. What is a psychic dimension? It's a conceptual perspective. Quantum mechanics speaks of collapsing a probability wave to find either the speed or the location of a proton. We can likewise speak – *by way of analogy* – of a clinical repressed unconscious – as we might speak of mind in general – as a world of probability waves. That is, a world of many possibilities awaiting concrete experience through observation, that is, interpretation. No wonder Bion suggests one should come to each session without memory or desire; such a suggestion is consonant with a worldview of high probability rather than repeatable, measurable determinism.

Our everyday accepted notions of mind assume a singularity that, in fact, is not reflective of reality. In a previous publication (Gargiulo, 2004), I noted:

> We come to know mind through all the languages of culture. It is, consequently, not reducible to a biological entity. Consciousness, which is uniquely dependent on neurological brain functioning, is a prerequisite for the experience of mind, but it is not co-equal. Consciousness, in human experience, makes the awareness of mind possible. But meaning, which is the calling card of mind, so to speak, is a singularly communal accomplishment.
>
> (p. 35)

And further, "Meaning is a communal experience on a social as well as singular scale; in a psychoanalytic experience it is dependent on all of what each participant brings – given their personal, social, familial, and cultural histories" (p. 36). Our experience of mind is always in the present – all that exits is the present – notwithstanding the apparent seductions of memory.[21] Memory, as we know, is not an indelible photograph or digital recording; it cannot be captured as we might capture images or sounds on an iPhone. Memories, as we know, are constantly evolving and changing. Therefore, what an analyst or patient focuses on determines what she or he will find – but the finding, of necessity, is always a new edition. That is, a re-creation of a memory, a feeling, or a phantasy. One finds what is already there awaiting to be found. To repeat, the past is constantly being recreated and consequently re-experienced – *as a new edition* – depending on who and where we are, and what is going on in the present.[22] What I have mentioned here – as obvious as it is – is, I believe, equally applicable to the psychoanalytic understanding of transference and countertransference. Transference, as we know, is not a literal replaying of a past experience – not an exact replication but rather better understood as a re-creation – created by both patient and analyst (as is countertransference). All we have is the now;[23] a now that is shadowed by the past but not, necessarily, over-shadowed by it.

In summary, what we refer to as a patient's unconscious – as elaborated and explored in therapy – comes *to be* through an interpretive process. In all the many defenses we use, and which psychoanalysis has studied, that is, splitting, denial, projection, and so on, most of what we discover is a result of our naming them as such. We are constantly elaborating our sense of self, rethinking our self-image, our hopes, and our fears, using our imagination – an imagination that is not bound by time, easily entertains opposites, and can easily reverse cause and effect. An imagination that is a deep well of creativity, personal, poetic, and scientific.[24] (Einstein had extensive correspondence with Freud and highly praised his writing style, but he did not subscribe to his theories – he speaks of imagination, not of an unconscious.) As we know, helping a patient see how he or she manages what is painful is one of the most productive functions of the psychoanalytic processes. Such a process makes possible to tap the roots of memories or denied or split off emotional reactions or phantasies. What we refer to as the repressed unconscious is split off awareness. That is, it signals the capacity we humans have to be both aware and unaware at the same time; to turn our awareness away from what we experience as painful or disruptive. We can speak of repression as a counterforce or as a consequence of splitting. How one structures a quantum observation depends on both knowledge and imagination – the same is equally true in psychoanalytic clinical practice. The consequent "findings" between analyst and patient reflect such a process as well. *The questions one asks dictate the answers one receives.* The repressed unconscious is, as we have mentioned, an experienced reality, but it is not a mental warehouse of archeological finds.[25] Rather, the term "unconscious" points to a dynamic mental function (i.e., repression), as Freud summarizes in *The Ego and the Id.*[26]

Clinical Dynamics

Because the operational models of transference and countertransference are so basic to psychoanalytic practice, allow me to recap how I see the benefit of quantum models in reference to such. We cannot relive the past; only the present is open to us. Just as a proton only exists when it is observed, similarly, what we identify as the past exists when it is experienced as a present creation. The concept of a proton has to be clari-fied; that is, a proton is a point of reference – the term reflects just an excitation in an energy field. It is dynamic, not structural. Transference is a lived new creation, not a historical duplication; notwithstanding that its ingredients obviously have deep historical roots. Patients bring their needs, desires, hopes, memories, and ways of relating to the analytic setting. To what extent one might wish to view a patient as created by the therapeutic encounter, or not, is not the focus of this discussion. *Our knowledge of a proton is a result of interactive observation, likewise our knowledge of a patient – that is what makes transference so valuable.* To continue our analogy, transference might also be likened to a probability wave. When it is observed – that is, measured/observed, that is, inter-preted – it manifests itself as concrete phenomena. *Nothing, as we know, can be an exact replication of anything else.* The experience of transfer-ence, to repeat, is a new experience, but one deeply informed by personal history.[27] Of course, all a person's prior relationships (particularly early developmental primary relationships) color present experience; this is another way of saying that we are historical creatures as we experience our ongoing creation in the present. Psychoanalysis has the possibility of giving us a new history, as mentioned by Ricoeur, via expanded memories and alternate interpretations.[28] It may even go deeper than this, but lan-guage fails us at a certain point.

Entanglement

Within the quantum universe (the micro realm) we have additional oddi-ties . . . bedeviling Einstein and again offering *productive comparisons* to psychoanalytic experience. Take a pair of related protons and separate one from the other by any distance. *When the directional spin of one proton is changed, you can be assured that the directional spin of the other changes simultaneously, no matter the distance between them. Such a phenomenon is called entanglement.*[29] We are not sure how it works, but the fact that it does work has been validated, repeatedly. Einstein called such a find-ing "spooky action at a distance" since the entangled particles appear to communicate at a faster-than-light-speed. (This was Einstein's difficulty.) One alternate explanation (Gisin, 2014) suggests that distance, or better yet locality, does not exist, except possibly as something we might be imposing, something we construct via our perceptions. As mentioned, this behavior of protons is referred to as entanglement.

By way of suggestive *analogy*, we might ask: are two individuals connected in the same therapeutic place somehow, like the phenomena of two related protons, that is, which are entangled? Are all humans possibly entangled? Might such a possibility help explain what we refer to as unconscious communication? We can note here Whitehead's conviction (Whitehead, 1957) that every atom in the universe relates to every other atom in the universe. Following Whitehead's lead, we note that to interact with another, to create anything for another, is to create oneself simultaneously as well.[30] Is this possibly a theoretical model for the clinical work of Theodor Reik, Ferenczi, and others? Freud's interest in telepathy may not have been just a personal idiosyncrasy, but an intuition of something he sensed but did not have a model for by which to understand – something that quantum models help clarify.

Theodor Reik (1948) believed that to know another's clinical unconscious, one had to know and trust one's own. Such an approach is more than difficult to explain if we are all distinct and separate individuals. It is not possible if we are not, in some way, connected with each other. Hans Loewald (2000) spoke to this when he wrote: "Our object, being what it is, is the other in ourselves and ourselves in the other. To discover truth about the patient is always discovering it with him and for him as well as for ourselves and about ourselves" (p. 297). Our current Western culture assumes and aggravates subject/object, self/other distinctions. Might the brilliant quantum physicist Edwin Schrödinger (1983) be correct in following the conviction of the ancient Upanishads? That is, that there might be only one consciousness; our individual consciousness would then be simply participatory. Might such ancient Hindu beliefs, as well our Western Spinoza, have had it right? That is, that in some profound way, we are all one?[31] There are respected quantum physicists who suggest such a possibility.[32]

Is reality one or many? Clearly it is both. It bears repeating that the uniqueness of the therapeutic encounter and consequently its nonrepeatability is not a negative, as is implied in Newtonian scientific models. It is, given certain parameters, similar to the type of observation evidenced in quantum physics observations. *The questions we ask determine the answers we get* is just as true for psychoanalysis as it is for physics.

Cause and Effect

Finally, another more than puzzling observation from quantum physics that can be seen as paralleling clinical experience is the finding that the usual sequence of cause and effect is not absolute. What does that mean? Basically, as John Wheeler demonstrated in his *delayed choice experiment*, a later adjustment of a phenomenon can change a prior setting; that is, under certain conditions, *if one changes the effect, one can modify the cause*.[33] Obviously this is not something we live within our everyday macro world. Consequently, causes and effects, in the micro world, are not sequentially absolute – they are relative. Might such a finding on the possibility of modifying an effect and consequently changing the cause be a suggestive *analogy*, to explore Paul Ricoeur's (1970) thought that psychoanalysis can give a patient a new history? Wheeler's delayed choice experiment suggests that the past can be effected by the future (see Rosenblum and Kuttner, 2011, pp. 87–99). To repeat, re-interpreted thoughts, feelings, and/or phantasies can change one's history. To change the effect is to change the cause; recreating the past anew, in therapy, has the possibility of changing ghosts into ancestors, as Loewald (1960) reminds us, giving a patient a new experienced history – one experienced within the wider context of fuller awareness.[34] Rovelli (2018) notes, "There is no single time: there is a different duration for every trajectory; and time passes at different rhythms according to place and according to speed. It is not directional: the difference between past and future does not exist in the elementary equations of the world" (p. 91). I am not suggesting planting new memories in patients; rather, more often than not, as an ongoing analysis proceeds, a patient remembers a wider context to their experiences. Such a wider context – generating new emotions – is the possible ground space for what is meant by analysis giving a patient a new history, as I read Ricoeur.

Final Thought

Quantum phenomena are unknowable in the usual meaning of knowable. All we know of the quantum world are our descriptions of it, as Niels Bohr reminds us, not the quantum realm itself. Likewise, with our everyday experience of reality: is what we name as reality, at its basic foundational level, simply made up of energy fields, or alternately, of tiny strings? What are strings but vibrations at different frequencies? Might such strings be the ultimate structure of the cosmos? Unknown. Might we, in our universe, be one of multi-universes? We don't know.[35] Might what we experience as reality possibly be a hologram? For some noted physicists, such a hologram is a defensible possibility.[36] Finally, we might note that Kant was half right – we cannot know the "thing-in-itself" – all we know are our descriptions. Ultimately, we construct the world we live in. The quantum world, despite it being the most validated scientific theory, exists – in our experience – as a theoretical construct. What ultimately seems most basic to our understanding of the world is information. Pagels (1982) notes that quantum energy fields manifest information.

In summary, I have used some findings from quantum physics to deepen our understanding of basic clinical experiences. For one, what we name as the repressed unconscious is co-created in the present, not simply excavated from a past. The past of memory is the articulated present. What we find of the past is created in the present by interpretation. Of course, what is found is waiting to be created – just like a proton is waiting, so to speak, to be observed. All we have is the present. Note Damasio (2012): "As lived experiences are reconstructed and replayed, whether in conscious reflection or in unconscious processing, their substance is reassessed and inevitably rearranged, modified minimally or very much in terms of their factual composition and emotional accompaniment" (pp. 223–224). Damasio then quotes T.S. Eliot to underline his position: "Time past and time future/What might have been and what has been/point to one end, which is always present" (p. 315).

New models can both enlighten as well as confuse. At their best they can stimulate thought, imagination, and creativity – all of which can open new vistas and pathways. A discipline grows as it is able to sustain itself with open dialogue with other disciplines. What I have offered here is in the service of greater dialogue.

Notes

1 Whether and if psychoanalysis is a science and if so, what kind, and if not, why not, is not addressed in this communication. Ricoeur and Grunbaum, among others, have discussed such issues. I am addressing some clinical experiences that, in process, can be broadly considered scientific. Meaning, they have a parallel in how we have come to learn the quantum realm.

 2 Niels Bohr (2010/1961) notes: "Indeed, the necessity of considering the inter-action between the measuring instruments and the object under investigation in atomic mechanics exhibits a close analogy to the peculiar difficulties in psychological analysis arising from the fact that the mental content is invariably altered when the attention is concentrated on any special feature of it" (p. 11).

 3 One of the basic findings of quantum physics is that there is no objective, self-sustaining world out there; meaning, seemingly, that it does not exist, if not observed. This is the classical Copenhagen interpretation. Alternately, Everett's multiple world(s) theory does away with any need for some form of observation. See Carroll (2019).

 4 See Rovelli (2021) for an extensive discussion of this conclusion.

 5 Rovelli (2018) adds in a footnote: "The technical term for interaction used in this context, 'measure' is misleading because it seems to imply that in order to create reality, we need an experimental physicist in a white coat." (p. 89).

 6 Note D'Espagnat (2006): while "in classical physics the laws were objectively interpretable – they supposedly described what exists – in quantum physics they are but observational predictive rules" (p. 225).

 7 Notwithstanding Einstein's (1961) conviction that God did not play dice with the world, his theories of relativity clearly show that we only know universals when and only when we know particular context: "Every reference-body (co-ordinate system) has its own particular time; unless we are told the reference-body to which the statement of time refers, there is no meaning in a statement of the time of an event" (p. 31).

 8 See, for example, Will and Yunes (2020), as well as Rovelli (2018) and his lists of Einstein's errors.

 9 Freud (1965a), Chapter XII. It was Freud's belief that nothing in the mind is arbitrary or undetermined.

10 See Damasio (2012): "Our memories are prejudiced, in the full sense of the term, by our history and beliefs. Perfectly faithful memory is a myth, applicable only to trivial objects. The notion that the brain ever holds anything like an isolated 'memory of the object' seems untenable" (p. 142). See Dehaene (2020): "[E]ach restored memory is a reconstruction: remembering is attempting to play back the very same neuronal firing pattern that occurred in the same brain circuits during a past experience" (p. 90).

11 Damasio (2012). Obviously, there is what Damasio categorizes as the cognitive unconscious as well as the genetic unconscious and what he names the genomic unconscious, which account for all the biological, neurological, and intellectual functions we perform non-consciously (pp. 294–301). Likewise, Dehaene (2014): "A wild profusion of unconscious processors weaves the texture of who we are and how we act" (p. 191).

12 Dehaene (2014).

13 Freud (2005) continues, "an existing living thing capable of development, and it maintains number of other relations with the pcs, including co-operation . . . it constantly influences – and, conversely, is even subject to influences from – the pcs." Roy Schafer (1981) spoke to the issue of reifying the unconscious as well. Francois Roustang (1996) proposes that Freud's unconscious has the same reality as one's imagination and that they are one and the same (p. 164).

14 Solms (2021) adds to this definition by the following: "Given my definition of consciousness as felt uncertainty, it is also interesting to note the role of surprisal in aesthetic experience" (p. 236).

15 As Rosenblum and Kuttner (2011) note: "The waviness in a region . . . is the probability that the object will be found in that region. The probability interpretation of waviness is central to the Copenhagen interpretation" (p. 128).

16 For a complementary reading of the extensive non-conscious functions of the brain, see Dehaene (2014). The psychoanalytic understanding of such defenses as repression, denial, and splitting help us conceptualize what I am referring to as the clinical unconscious.

17 A proton that behaves like a wave but also as if it were a discrete object . . . such a state of being is referred to as *superposition*. Richard Feynman famously noted that no one understands the quantum world. It is known through our human lens – a very limited and narrow lens.

18 Defining consciousness is a constant source of puzzlement. The philosopher Chalmers (1996) notes that "we do not know what consciousness is," while the neurologist Dehaene (2014) defines consciousness as "brain-wide information sharing" (p. 161, ff).

19 Gargiulo (2016), p. 27. (See also note 13.)

20 I am indebted to Andre Green (1975) for stimulating my thoughts, i.e., "in the end the real analytic object is neither on the patient's side nor on the analyst's but in the meeting . . . in the potential space between them. . . . The analyst does not only unveil a hidden meaning. He constructs a meaning which has never been created before the analytic relationship began" (p. 12A). Bohr (2010) notes "the impossibility of providing an unambiguous content to the idea of subconsciousness corresponds to the impossibility of pictorial interpretation of the quantum-mechanical formalism" (p. 77).

21 For an extensive and insightful discussion of mind, see Cavell (1988).

22 Gargiulo (2008): "Memory is as selective as perception itself is. Memory, all too often, is a child of desire. What we experience as reality depends on the meaning, we give it. We are children of the language our culture speaks . . . there are many cultures and many languages" (p. 137).

23 Ogden (1994) speaks of the *present moment of the past* (p. 61). We are all aware of the masterful weaving of remembered past and present that Jorge Luis Borges portrays.

24 Barfield (2019) notes: "If we view the imagination as an isolated, self-involved faculty, creating artifacts that are irrelevant to our discovery of reality, we will never grasp its significance" (p. 144).

25 Francois Roustang (1996) maintains, as mentioned, that the foundational model of the clinical unconscious is the imagination. Roustang sees no need to posit anything additional as a biological or theoretical modality for an such an unconscious (p. 164).

26 *The Ego and the Id* (1960): "[W]e restrict the term unconscious to the dynamically unconscious repressed" (p. 6). While in *New Introductory Lectures* (1965b), speaking generically of what is unconscious, he writes: "In both cases we have to reckon with the disagreeable discovery that on the one hand

(super)ego and conscious and on the other hand repressed and unconscious are far from coinciding" (p. 86).

27 Note Hoffman's (2021) comment: "Interestingly enough, the concept of transference has been demonstrated experimentally by social cognitive psychologists, who have concluded that in ordinary social encounters, prior relationships do play an important role in contemporary relationships" (p. 105).

28 See Ricoeur (1970).

29 Entanglement is being studied continuously. For a basic introduction see Aczel's (2001) text entitled *Entanglement*. Carroll's (2019) text also discusses entanglement extensively. Brody (2020) reiterates the Copenhagen interpretation: "measurement creates objectively real states" (p. 83). And, by way of analogy, we are understanding interpretation as measurement. See also Berkowitz (2021) for continuous verification of entanglement.

30 Note Mitchel and Staretz (2011): "Like it or not, we appear to live in a participatory universe – there is no such thing as pure objective reality, and we influence everything that we interact with. Perhaps this is the same mechanism why we 'feel' positive energy from some people while others seem to emit negative energy?" (p. 942).

31 See Gargiulo (2018).

32 Carroll (2016).

33 This refers to the delayed choice experiment. See Rosenblum and Kuttner (2011) (p. 153): "The 'delayed-choice experiment' suggested by quantum cosmologist John Wheeler comes closest to testing the backward-in-time aspect of quantum theory. It confirmed the prediction of quantum theory that an observation creates the relevant history."

34 Note Hans Loewald's (1960) brilliant insight that at the end of a successful analysis, ghosts have been transformed into ancestors reflect the same goal. "In the daylight of analysis, the ghosts of the unconscious are laid and let to rest as ancestors whose power is taken over and transformed into the newer intensity of present life, of the secondary process and contemporary objects" (p. 28).

35 Kaku (2021). See his discussion of string theory.

36 Leonard Susskind, the author of *The Black Hole War* (2008), has written and lectured (Ted Talks) on this possibility.

References

Aczel, A. (2001). *Entanglement*. New York: Penguin Publications.

Barfield, R. (2019). *The Poetic Apriori*. Stuttgart: Ibidem.

Berkowitz, R. (2021). Macroscopic systems can be controllably entangled and limitlessly measured. *Physics Today, 74*(7), 16–18.

Bohr, N. (2010/1961). *Atomic Physics and Human Knowledge*. New York: Dover Publications, Inc.

Brody, J. (2020). *Quantum Entanglement*. Cambridge, MA: The MIT Press.

Carroll, S. (2016). *The Big Picture*. New York: Random House.

————. (2019). *Something Deeply Hidden*. New York: Random House.

Cavell, M. (1988). Solipsism and community. *Psychoanalysis and Contemporary Thought*, 11(4).

Chalmers, D. (1996). *The Conscious Mind*. New York. Oxford University Press.

Damasio, A. (2012). *Self Comes to Mind*. New York: Vintage Books.

Dehaene, S. (2014). *Consciousness and the Brain*. New York: Penguin Books.

————. (2020). *How We Learn*. New York: Viking.

D'Espagnat, B. (2006). *On Physics and Philosophy*. Princeton: Princeton University Press.

Einstein, A. (1929). In Viereck, G. *Viereck's Interview With Einstein*. The Saturday Evening Post.

Einstein, A. (1961). *Relativity*. New York: Three Rivers Press. The Saturday Evening Post, November Issue.

Freud, S. (1922). *Beyond the Pleasure Principle*. Mansfield Centre, CT: Martino, 2009.

————. (1960). *The Ego and the Id*. New York: W.W. Norton.

————. (1965a). *The Psychopathology of Everyday Life*. New York: W.W. Norton & Co.

————. (1965b). *New Introductory Lectures on Psycho-Analysis*. New York: W.W. Norton. (Strachey Ed)

————. (2005). *The Unconscious*. New York: Penguin Books. (Graham Frankland, Translator)

Gargiulo, G. J. (2004). *Psyche, Self and Soul*. London: Whurr Publishers.

————. (2008). *Broken Fathers/Broken Sons*. New York: Rodopi Publications.

————. (2016). *Quantum Psychoanalysis: Essays on Physics, Mind, and Analysis Today*. New York: International Psychoanalytic Books.

————. (2018). Einstein, time and the unconscious. *The Psychoanalytic Review*, 105(1) (February), 119–124.

Gisin, N. (2014). *Quantum Chance*. Geneva, Switzerland: Springer Publications.

Green, A. (1975). The analyst, symbolization, and absence in the analytic setting. *International Journal of Psychoanalysis*, 56, 1–22.

Hawking, S. W. (2002). *The Theory of Everything*. Beverly Hills, CA: New Millennium Press.

Heisenberg, W. (1958/1999). *Physics and Philosophy*. New York: Prometheus Books.

Hoffman, I. Z. (2021). Evolution of a "classic" psychoanalytic institute. *The Psychoanalytic Review*, 108(1), 97–120.

Kaku, M. (2021). *The God Equation: The Quest for a Theory of Everything*. New York: Doubleday.

Kumar, M. (2008). *Quantum*. New York: W.W. Norton & Co.

Loewald, H. (1960). On the therapeutic action of psycho-analysis. *International Journal of Psychoanalysis*, 41, 16–33.

Loewald, W. H. (2000). *The Essential Loewald*. Hagerstown, MD: University Publishing Group.

Mitchel, E. & Staretz, R. (2011). The quantum hologram and the nature of consciousness. In *Consciousness and The Universe*. Cambridge, MA: Cosmology Science Publishers.

Ogden, T. H. (1994). *Subjects of Analysis*. London: Karnac Books.

Pagels, H. (1982). *The Cosmic Code*. New York: Simon and Schuster.

Reik, T. (1936). *Surprise and The Psychoanalyst*. New York: Routledge.

————. (1948). *Listening with the Third Ear*. New York: Grove Press.

Ricoeur, P. (1970). *Freud and Philosophy*. New Haven: Yale University Press.

Rosenblum, B. & Kuttner, F. (2011). *Quantum Enigma*. Second edition. New York: Oxford University Press.

Roustang, F. (1996). *How to Make a Paranoid Laugh or, What is Psychoanalysis?* Philadelphia: University of Pennsylvania Press.

Rovelli, C. (2018). *The Order of Time*. New York: Riverhead Books.

————. (2021). *Helgoland: Making Sense of the Quantum Revolution* (E. Segre and S. Carnell, Translators). New York: Riverhead Books (Original work published in 2020).

Schafer, R. (1981). *Action Language*. New Haven: Yale University Press.

Schrödinger, E. (1983). *My View of the World*. New York: Cambridge University Press.

Solms, M. (2021). *The Hidden Spring*. New York: W.W. Norton & Co.

Susskind, L. (2008). *The Black Hole War*. New York: Little, Brown and Co.

Whitehead, A. N. (1957). *Process and Reality*. New York: Harper and Row.

Will, C. & Yunes, N. (2020). *Is Einstein Still Right?* Oxford: Oxford University Press.

Chapter 2

Psychoanalysis and Physics
A Quantum Sensibility

John Turtz, PhD

"The doorstep to the temple of wisdom is a knowledge of our own ignorance."

Charles Haddon Spurgeon (1922)

"The most beautiful experience we can have is the mysterious. It is the fundamental emotion which stands at the cradle of true art and true science."

Albert Einstein (1930)

Lakoff and Johnson (1980) have demonstrated that metaphors "structure how we perceive, how we think, and what we do" (p. 4). Metaphor underpins our conceptual structures and our capacity for reason. Gargiulo (2016) has written, "Minimally we can say that unless we are constantly refinding the metaphorical aspect of our knowledge, we can, all too easily, slip into a literal, concrete understanding of it" (p. 84). By this, Gargiulo means that creating new metaphors for the psychoanalytic process is vital to keeping psychoanalysis alive. This chapter will explore new metaphors that can be appropriated from quantum physics. These new metaphors in turn can expand our perceptions and our frameworks for understanding the human beings that we work so closely with.

An apocryphal quote attributed to Einstein is: "As our circle of knowledge expands, so does the circumference of darkness surrounding it." I have always appreciated the image conjured up by these words, and it seems apt, then, that after all of the extraordinary achievements in physics over the past five centuries, we have become aware of the fact that 96 percent of the universe is made up of dark energy and dark matter, which we know next to nothing about. In a similar vein, even with all we have learned about

DOI: 10.4324/9781003271499-4

neuroscience and the human brain, we still cannot definitively state what consciousness is and how it is generated. Given the remarkable achievements in human knowledge since the advent of the Scientific Revolution, we sometimes forget just how little we know and how much we need to tolerate humility and admit to ignorance in order to learn.

There is an old story about an inebriated man who drops his keys at night and then searches for them in the circle of light formed by a nearby lamppost, not because that is where the keys necessarily were dropped, but because that is where the light is. I sometimes wonder if we psychoanalysts focus a bit too much on the circle of light that encompasses current psychoanalytic knowledge and not enough on the surrounding darkness. Moving outside our circle of psychoanalytic knowledge and plunging into the unchartered waters of the unknown can, in my view, greatly enhance our work.

Quantum physics has been one such area of exploration for me, an area of unfamiliar waters that has increased my sense of wonder and broadened my limited horizons. Quantum mechanics is the study of the subatomic world and how subatomic particles move and interact. The psychoanalyst William Coburn (2014) refers to what he calls a "complexity sensibility" when writing of the magical world of complexity theory (the study of nonlinear dynamic systems) and its relationship to psychoanalytic work. I wish to discuss what I am calling a *quantum sensibility* and hope to demonstrate how the mysterious world of quantum physics has applicability to psychoanalysis.

In 1905, Einstein broke through the world of physics with four revolutionary papers, including one on the theory of special relativity and a paper that brings to light (no pun intended!) the most famous mathematical equation in history: $E = mc^2$. His paper on the photoelectric effect and the particle nature of light, however, is the one that won him the Nobel Prize and the one that helped give birth to the field of quantum mechanics, which Einstein ironically ended up debating against for the rest of his life.

Quantum physics focuses on what is termed the microworld, the world of subatomic particles. How can this possibly relate to the macroworld, the world of our everyday experience and the world in which we analysts do our work? This is the question I have been asked on numerous occasions, and this is the question I wish to explore in this chapter. The following are some of my recent reflections on physics, philosophy and psychoanalysis; I hope to demonstrate how these reflections have spawned in me a quantum sensibility.

Plato's Allegory of the Cave

The interpersonal psychoanalyst Edgar Levenson (1996) begins one of his papers with an epigraph, a quotation from the novelist Jane Smiley: "Appearances aren't deceiving, I think, but you have to know where to look" (p. 1). As an analyst heavily influenced by interpersonal and existential/phenomenological theory, I have always appreciated this quote. As with Levenson (1981), I tend to focus on the truth and reality of an individual's experience, both past and present, and view "distortion" more from a lens of poorly comprehended experience than from the framework of an intrapsychic and autonomous fantasy process. On the other hand, however, delving into the philosophical consequences of the science of quantum mechanics brings to mind not Smiley's quote, but Plato's Allegory of the Cave. Plato, through the voice of Socrates of course, told the parable of prisoners chained in a cave with their heads immobile, so that they could only stare at the wall in front of them. Behind them is a fire, and between the fire and the prisoners is an area where people can walk and hold up figures of various objects. The light from the fire hitting these figures casts shadows upon the cave wall, and the prisoners take these shadows to be reality because it is all they can observe and experience. These shadows on the cave wall are in actuality just that – shadows of the ultimate reality that lies behind the prisoners and of which they are totally unaware. This allegory was used by Plato to illuminate his Theory of Forms.

Quantum mechanics compels us to question what appears as reality to our human senses and our human mind. We are creatures that evolved to survive in the macroworld; the underlying structure of the microworld of subatomic particles and the fundamental nature of reality are inherently counterintuitive. Complementarity, the dual wave-particle nature of light, is just one of many examples of the counterintuitive nature of reality at the fundamental level.

So, at a minimum, contemporary physics upends much of our commonsense understanding of the world and the ultimate nature of reality, and it profoundly impacts our underlying ontological and epistemological philosophies. The great quantum physicist Niels Bohr himself said, "Anyone who is not shocked by quantum theory has not understood it" (as cited in Barad, 2007, p. 254). Bernard d'Espagnat (2006), a theoretical physicist with a strong foundation in philosophy, asserts that reality is of two orders: (1) empirical reality and (2) veiled reality, which we can catch glimpses of but never fully grasp. And the physicist David Bohm (1980) refers to the implicate and the explicate order, the implicate order being a more fundamental order of reality than the explicate order, which refers to the order of human perception and abstraction. It seems unimaginable to me that someone could explore the concepts emerging from contemporary physics and *not* be shaken up to some degree. It is like entering Wonderland or, more accurately, like suddenly realizing you've always been living in Wonderland without knowing it. The world becomes topsy-turvy, and reality begins to feel illusory. Quantum physics may not spawn as abrupt a revolution as the Copernican Revolution or the Einsteinian Revolution, but it is a revolution nonetheless, a major paradigm shift that has both profound metaphorical and literal consequences for philosophy, psychoanalysis and our view of our place in the universe. Some of these implications for psychoanalysis are as follows:

- The inseparable connection between the observer and the observed: In psychoanalysis, this is reflected in the convergence of all major psychoanalytic orientations to a two-person psychology, initiated by psychoanalysts such as Sullivan with his concept of participant-observation.
- The paradigm shift from certainty and a deterministic clockwork universe to a model of indeterminacy and probabilistic statistics: In psychoanalysis, this was illustrated early on by the Sullivanian notion that there are no absolute truths, only successive approximations. This Sullivanian concept has blossomed into the work of such notable psychoanalysts as Edgar Levenson, Irwin Hirsch and Donnel Stern.
- The movement from reductionism to holism and the crucial importance of relational interactions.
- The idea that there is much mystery beyond our magnificent yet feeble human strivings: This great unknown can be anxiety-provoking and perhaps even overwhelming at times, but what a desolate life this would be without mystery! The exploration of physics has a humbling influence upon us, leading to experiences of awe and reverence. I believe that this attitude of humility can only benefit us as we stumble along the path of psychoanalysis, for certainty is the enemy of psychoanalysis.

The Quantum Unconscious

Gargiulo (2016) views what, in the Copenhagen interpretation of quantum mechanics, is called the collapse of the wavefunction as a metaphor for the role of interpreting unconscious phenomena. In order to better understand what the collapse of the wavefunction is, we need to first delve into the concept of complementarity, that is, the dual wave-particle nature of light. Thomas Young's famous double-slit experiment beautifully illustrates this. If photons of light are shot through an open slit in a thin metal sheet, a uniform distribution of dots appears on a photographic plate behind the metal sheet. This is what would be expected given the nature of particles.

If the same experiment is then run again, but with two open slits instead of one, the pattern of dots changes. One then finds dark bands where numerous photons have struck the photographic plate and light bands where only a few photons have struck. This is called an interference pattern and only occurs when waves interfere with each other. Therefore, with one slit open the photons act like particles, but with two slits open they act like waves. But wait – it gets even stranger. If individual photons are shot one at a time through the two open slits, an interference pattern again emerges! How is this possible? That would mean that each photon passes through both slits simultaneously in a wavelike manner. And that, rather remarkably, is exactly what appears to occur. The photon enters what is termed a superposition state, whereby it is in more than one position at the same time! In actuality, prior to measurement, the particle is everywhere and nowhere at the same time. According to the Copenhagen interpretation, it is the measurement that collapses the wavefunction and allows for the particle to exist in a particular location in "reality." Therefore, it is the measurement that creates the particle. At the most fundamental level of reality, according to what is called quantum field theory, we appear to be dealing with quantum fields, not actual concrete particles. This begins to sound like a real-life version of Plato's Allegory of the Cave.

Before focusing on the meaning of the collapse of the wavefunction, let's first define what a wavefunction is. Rosenblum and Kuttner (2011) define the wavefunction as "the mathematical representation of the wave" (p. 77). The wavefunction, discovered by the physicist Erwin Schrödinger, is, in mathematical form, the probability of finding a subatomic particle in a certain location following a measurement. According to the Copenhagen interpretation of quantum mechanics, the measurement itself is said to collapse the wavefunction; collapsing the wavefunction means that one can now determine and pinpoint a specific location for the subatomic particle from all its possible locations. Before the measurement, there is only a "mist of infinite possibilities," to borrow the physicist John Wheeler's phrase (Wheeler, as cited in Gargiulo, 2016, p. 7). In an analogous manner, Gargiulo is proposing that prior to a psychoanalytic interpretation, there is only a mist of infinite possibilities; the interpretation then creates the reality. We are not referring to discovery here, as in Freud's concept of discovering the bedrock of a repressed truth; we are talking about creating, or rather co-creating and co-constructing truth between the analyst and analysand. This implies that meaning, prior to interpretation, is in a probability state, just as the position or momentum of a subatomic particle is a probability state. Taken to the nth degree, this in turn can only signify that there is no ultimate meaning. All interpretation can do is co-create with the analysand a highly probable meaning, which may help the patient increase his or her level of openness, spontaneity and growth. A shift to probabilistic thinking leads to seeing truth as approached only through successive approximation, as Sullivan understood.

If movement from unconscious to conscious experience were, at least metaphorically, analogous to what occurs in the collapse of the wavefunction, why would this be at all significant? How does all this abstract physics and philosophy affect us in our ordinary lives and in the consulting room? Perhaps most importantly, this helps us to understand that there is no ultimate truth; the bedrock of truth that Freud so intently pursued would be as illusory as the pot of gold at the end of the rainbow. Using metaphors from quantum mechanics, perspectivalism and indeterminacy take preference over absolute truth and certainty. And truth is co-created in dialogue rather than discovered by an objective observer digging for the bedrock of truth (as in Freud's archeological model, using Newtonian mechanics as its underlying foundation).

Let's take these concepts from quantum mechanics even further by exploring another interpretation of quantum mechanics. There are several interpretations of quantum mechanics other than the Copenhagen interpretation, the first interpretation of quantum physics and the one developed by the Danish physicist Niels Bohr. The American physicist Hugh Everett developed an even stranger interpretation. Everett originated what is called the Many Worlds interpretation of quantum mechanics. This model proposes that there is no such thing as a wavefunction collapse; rather, each possible collapse of a wavefunction (that occurs with a measurement) actually branches out into a different parallel universe. All possibilities transpire, but we can only be aware of what occurs in the branch of the universe that we are linked to. As outlandish as this sounds, this is what the mathematics of the wavefunction demonstrates, and more and more physicists, including Sean Carroll (2019), are coming to understand the cosmos in just this manner. The physicist Chad Orzel (2019), on the other hand, believes in the mathematics of the Many Worlds interpretation, but thinks the name of this model should be changed to the "Metaphorical Worlds Interpretation." The universe is one universal wavefunction; the branches, from Orzel's perspective, are metaphorical – they represent which subparts of the whole we decide to measure, but the universe itself is just that – one singular, whole universe. This model presents an apt metaphor with regard to the dissociative model of the unconscious (as contrasted with the repression model), particularly with individuals who have suffered from a history of severe trauma. These individuals can experience very compartmentalized and dissociated self-states. These are individuals that cannot, in Bromberg's words, "stand in the spaces between realities without losing any of them" (Bromberg, 1993, p. 166). For these individuals, what can emerge in one self-state is like a universe unto itself, a universe that has no way of communicating with other universes, that is, other self-states. What is "unconscious" is dependent on self-state. Think of different self-states as parallel universes. We are referring to the dissociative model of the unconscious in this context, not repression. In the case of psychoanalytic treatment, the goal is of course to develop co-communication, or *coconsciousness* (Howell, 2011), between different self-states, whereas in quantum physics, according to Everett's Many Worlds interpretation, these branching universes can never connect.

As one develops a quantum sensibility, one leaves the Newtonian world of certainty and absolute truth. Unconsciousness is simultaneously nothing and everything. This way of viewing "truth" lends support to the hermeneutic and Talmudic models of truth. Interpretation becomes a co-construction, mutually created by the analyst and analysand, as opposed to a discovery of an absolute truth; truth can never be fully realized.

Quantum Intersubjectivity

One of the twentieth century's most important scientific discoveries was Heisenberg's uncertainty principle. The uncertainty principle states that one cannot precisely measure both the position and momentum of a subatomic particle at the same time. The more one precisely measures position, the less information one can obtain with regard to momentum, and vice versa. How and what we observe impacts the results of the measurement, and this has nothing to do with the level of sophistication of our measuring instruments. Heisenberg's uncertainty principle thereby eradicates the idea of the pure objective observer. From Sullivan's early concept of participant-observation to the convergence of a two-person psychology in all contemporary psychoanalytic orientations, the direct and indirect influences of Heisenberg's principle appear to have made a significant impact upon psychoanalysis.

It seems to me that if there is no great divide between observer and observed (and therefore no great divide between mind and body as well as mind and world), then the dissociative model of the mind becomes the more powerful model as compared with the repression model of the unconscious. Dissociative processes are associated with what Donnel Stern terms *unformulated experience* (Stern, 1997), whereas repression refers to experience that has at one time been formulated but which was then repressed. The repression model leads the analyst toward digging deeply into the psyche for the bedrock of truth. With the dissociative model, we are dealing with successive approximations toward the truth, a truth that never becomes absolute (analogous to science itself). We are dealing with co-created enactments of unformulated experience, not observations of one human being by a neutral and objective observer. Hirsch (1994) has written, "Dissociation best fits the notion of consistent patterns of interpersonal experience and associated affects which may be entirely out of awareness yet are relived in the patient's subsequent relations, including the two-person playground of psychoanalysis" (pp. 779–780). Hirsch (1994) emphasizes the importance of enactment and sees the unconscious that is co-constructed through enactments as a relative unconscious in that it can never be fully known. The dissociated aspects of experience are always played out in the two-person system between the analyst and analysand, and in doing so reveal the "truth" in successive approximations.

Gargiulo (2016) notes that the concept of quantum entanglement is a wonderful metaphor for intersubjectivity and for the relational turn in psychoanalysis (Gargiulo, 2016). Quantum entanglement refers to what Einstein called "spooky action at a distance" (Rosenblum and Kuttner, 2011, p. 3). If a subatomic particle is split in two, the two new particles take on opposite spins. This occurs simultaneously, but it does not occur until a measurement is made. The moment in which the measuring instrument determines one particle's spin, the other particle *instantaneously* takes on the opposite spin. This occurs even when the particles are separated by great distance. And this experiment has actually been empirically validated. The question that bothered Einstein is the question of how these two particles could "communicate" in a manner seemingly faster than light speed, for there is nothing faster than the speed of light, according to the Special Theory of Relativity. We need to be careful of reifying this concept in a mystical manner, as many have done with concepts from quantum physics, but as a metaphor it does point toward the deep and profound form of relatedness that occurs when unconscious communication occurs between two individuals. It is also a wonderful metaphor for viewing the world as well as human nature and intersubjectivity from a holistic, as opposed to reductionist, perspective. As the physicist David Bohm wrote, "Ultimately, the entire universe (with all its 'particles,' including those constituting human beings, their laboratories, observing instruments, etc.) has to be understood as a single undivided whole, in which analysis into separately and independently existent parts has no fundamental status" (as cited in Grandy, 2009, p. 73).

The physicist Rovelli (2021) offers what he terms yet another interpretation of quantum mechanics: the *relational interpretation*. From this perspective, the focus is on interactions between objects, not on isolated objects themselves. Rovelli states if an object is not in interaction with another object in the cosmos, it has no properties and is for all essential purposes nonexistent. The world at its core "is a dense web of *interactions*" (Rovelli, 2020, p. 76), and "there are no properties outside of interactions" (Rovelli, 2020, p. 79). If Rovelli's relational interpretation of quantum mechanics is correct, then reality always emerges in interaction, and reality itself is relative; what is true for one object in interaction may not be the same truth for another object in a different interaction – this is the essence of the perspectival nature of reality. Perspectivalism becomes the essence of reality, as opposed to Newtonian predictability in a universe capable of being objectively observed in the search for fundamental and absolute truth. From the relational interpretation of quantum physics, reality is not discovered; it is created by which specific aspects of the universe and their interactions we choose to focus upon. In the psychoanalytic consulting room, reality is co-created in dialogue. It is difficult to come up with a better metaphor from quantum physics for the manner in which "truth" is lived out mutually in the interactions and enactments between analyst and analysand. What emerges in the interpersonal field between the analyst and analysand will be slightly different for each analyst-analysand pair. If everything exists only in relationship, then Rovelli's relational interpretation can be used to metaphorically reflect the co-construction of meaning that emerges in enactments in the interpersonal field between the analyst and analysand in the psychoanalytic consulting room.

Using the relational interpretation as a metaphor can also help the psychoanalyst move away from Cartesian thinking. Stolorow et al. (2002) have written about the impact of Descartes and Cartesian thinking on psychoanalysis. More specifically, they focus on several aspects of what they refer to as the Cartesian mind. The Cartesian mind is seen as a mind in "self-enclosed isolation" (Stolorow et al., 2002). It splits subject from object, mind from body, and internal psychic reality from external reality. The metaphors emanating from this philosophy are mechanistic ones and demonstrate clear boundaries between subject and object, as can be seen though such concepts as transference and countertransference, displacement and projective identification. Even in contemporary relational psychoanalysis, the remnants of the Cartesian worldview continue to persist (as in the concept of projective identification). The Cartesian mind is a disembodied, rational mind that is split off from emotional experience. This is the Enlightenment view of the mind. Freud focused on unconscious processes as opposed to conscious rationality, but he remained loyal to Cartesian philosophy by giving "the Cartesian house a basement, where the genuine sources of psychic life lived. Unfortunately, the Freudian unconscious is equally isolated and atomistic, mechanistic, inner, and subjective as the Cartesian mind" (Stolorow et al., p. 28). Stolorow et al. (2002) move away from the idea of Cartesian subjects and toward the concept of experiential worlds. The unconscious, seen from a more hermeneutic tradition, is seen metaphorically as limiting world horizons. This kind of phenomenological thinking does not see clearly demarcated boundaries between subject and object, inner and outer, conscious and unconscious. It is perspectival in thinking and sees minds not as isolated, but as interconnected via intersubjective fields that allow for emergence of novelty though nonlinear dynamic patterns of interaction. Letting go of Cartesian thinking leads to seeing minds not as isolated, disembodied and decontextualized, but as embodied and always emerging in intersubjective contexts. The relational interpretation of quantum physics, with its focus on interaction as opposed to isolated objects, can help to further facilitate this movement away from Cartesian thinking.

Quantum Existentialism

I have long been influenced by the concepts and ideas inherent in existentialism and existential psychoanalysis. When exploring quantum physics, I was struck by the affinity of some of its concepts to those of existential philosophy and existential psychoanalysis.

From the perspective of contemporary physics, our very existence itself is due to an accident – more specifically, it is due to the condensation of the Higgs field, an energy field that gives mass to objects in the universe (Krauss, 2017). The cosmos simply has no particular meaning or purpose for the human race. In this respect, there is an unexpected sense of familiarity between quantum physics and humanistic existentialism.

Human beings have come a long way from viewing ourselves as the center of the universe with a purpose designed for us. Copernicus, Darwin and Freud all played major roles in dethroning the human being. And now, from the perspective of contemporary physics, it appears that our existence has resulted from an accident. There simply is no inherent meaning to our human existence. We must create whatever meaning we bring to our existence. Quantum physics thereby offers support for humanistic existentialism's focus on the need for human beings to create their own meaning in a meaningless cosmos. As the existentialists emphasize, there is no blueprint, no essence to the human subject; the human individual always exists in the process of becoming. The radical sense of freedom can be rather terrifying; we create meaning through the choices we make as we live our lives and ultimately are responsible for those choices.

The Heisenberg uncertainty principle demonstrates the inseparability of subject and object. Quantum physics thereby also provides scientific support for existentialism's "endeavor to understand man by cutting below the cleavage between subject and object which has bedeviled Western thought and science since shortly after the Renaissance" (May et al., 1958, p. 11). According to May et al. (1958), this endeavor to heal the subject-object split is the defining factor of existentialism. The phenomenologist Edmund Husserl was one of the early philosophers to question Descartes' dualistic thinking. Husserl saw consciousness and the object of consciousness as simultaneously emerging together. Consciousness is always a pointing toward the object. "The nature of consciousness is to point beyond itself – to whatever datum it is conscious of. This is Husserl's basic doctrine of the *'intentionality'* of consciousness" (Barrett, 1979, p. 131). Along the same lines, Sartre saw consciousness as being "a negation of itself *toward* its object" (Barrett, 1979, p. 132). Therefore, by viewing the subject and object as inseparable, quantum mechanics supports existential philosophy and can play a significant role in the continuing attempt to heal the split between subject and object in Western philosophy.

From an existential perspective, truth is relational. May et al. (1958) quote Kierkegaard, the first existentialist:

> When the question of truth is raised in an objective manner, reflection is directed objectively to the truth, as an object to which the known is related. Reflection is not focused upon the relationship, however, but upon the question of whether it is the truth to which the knower is related. If only the object to which he is related is the truth, the subject is accounted to be in the truth. *When the question of the truth is raised subjectively, reflection is directed subjectively to the nature of the individual's relationship; if only the mode of this relationship is in the truth, the individual is in the truth, even if he should happen to be thus related to what is not true.*
>
> (p. 25)

No longer are we in the realm of the neutral scientist observing nature from a purely objective standpoint. We are in the realm of interactions and relationships. May et al. (1958) write, "Kierkegaard foretells the viewpoint of Bohr, Heisenberg, and other contemporary physicists that the Copernican view that nature can be separated from man is no longer tenable" (p. 26).

Truth emerges in relationship. Kierkegaard's concept of truth as relational not only anticipates Bohr and Heisenberg, but also Rovelli's contemporary relational interpretation of psychoanalysis. Rovelli's relational interpretation provides a perspective on the relational aspects of being and existence that is quite in accordance with and supportive of existential philosophy's concept of truth.

Both existentialism and quantum mechanics have an anti-reductionist perspective. Existential psychoanalysis sees human subjectivity and the nature of Being (in the Heideggerian sense) as irreducible. In a world where subjectivity is being lost and where an inner sense of agency is becoming less and less visible, the radical nature of freedom, agency and responsibility from an existential perspective can be a valuable counterweight to the postmodernist conception of the decentered self (Frie, 1997, 2002, 2003). Psychoanalysis from an existential and phenomenological tradition can play a significant role in not letting the human subject disappear into the mist of postmodern relativism. And concepts and models from quantum physics converge nicely with existentialism. Quantum physics' emphasis upon indeterminacy and holism and its challenge to the Newtonian paradigm's tenets of the subject-object split, the objective observer, determinism and reductionism provide corroboration for the underlying principles of existential philosophy and existential psychoanalysis.

Though perhaps just a bit tangential, I cannot resist the temptation to briefly touch upon the concept of time as it relates to physics and to the existential human condition. St. Augustine (trans. 1943) famously wrote in his *Confessions*, "What then, is time? If no one asks of me, I know; if I wish to explain to him who asks, I know not" (Book XI, Chapter XIV). Physicists offer various models as to what time really is, but at present physics offers no generally accepted and validated theory that explains the concept of time. We simply do not have a solid theoretical understanding of what time is. What we do know from physics, though, is that at the fundamental level of subatomic particles, there is no such thing as time. In the quantum microworld, the fundamental laws of physics are reversible. If you made a movie of the motions of subatomic particles, you would not be able discern playing this movie forward from playing it backward (as you would, for example, in watching a movie showing an egg being cracked or a glass object being broken). The only reason we even experience the flow of time at all in the macroworld is because our universe, right at the time of the big bang, was in an extremely low state of entropy and, as per the Second Law of Thermodynamics, has then been continuously moving toward a higher state of entropy ever since. In other words, the cosmos has been continuously moving toward greater and greater disorder since its origins. A cracked egg is not going to magically become whole again and move from a state of disorder to one of greater organization. It is only because our universe began as it did that we can remember the past while the future remains unknowable. This is what leads to the emergence of time in our macroworld. Time is therefore an emergent feature of our universe (as opposed to a fundamental aspect of the nature of reality). Existentialists emphasize a radical freedom and responsibility, the freedom to choose within the limits and constraints of one's *thrown condition*, that is, the historical time period, place and culture in which one is born. As an emergent feature of the universe, time plays a crucial factor in the creation of our human existential situation; it is time itself that underlies so many of the conundrums and dichotomies of human existence, including the existential issue of our mortality, as well as the limitations and constraints upon our lives that paradoxically are so critical to the emergence of free will.

Aliveness and Mystery

Above all, connecting with the mysteries of quantum physics and the mysteries of the cosmos has enriched my life and my clinical work in ways that are difficult to articulate, but I will do my best. It seems to me that by expanding one's external horizons, one naturally and inevitably expands one's internal horizons as well. And expanding our limited horizons, from a phenomenological perspective, is perhaps the core objective in a psychoanalytic treatment (Stolorow et al., 2002). Stolorow et al. (2002), greatly influenced by phenomenology, see "unconsciousness in terms of the limiting horizons of an experiential world" (p. 46) and see psychoanalysis as working toward "comprehension of the network of conviction, the rules of principles that prereflectively organize the patient's world and keep the patient's experiencing confined to its frozen horizons and limiting perspectives" (p. 46).

My exploration of quantum physics has not only expanded my knowledge and understanding, but has also exposed the limits to my knowledge. Learning, as implied in the opening of this chapter, is a humbling experience, and humility, so essential to learning, is also essential to working as a psychoanalyst. The capacity to tolerate uncertainty and *not* knowing, so crucial to our work, requires a sense of humility. Beware the analyst with a sense of certainty, the analyst that quickly sizes up a patient and fits that individual into the Procrustean bed of that analyst's theoretical stance. Erich Fromm (1947) wrote, "[T]he quest for certainty blocks the search for meaning" (p. 45). Exploring challenging areas outside of psychoanalysis can, in some ways, be a meditative practice in humility.

Perhaps most importantly, connecting with the mysteries of what we don't know inspires awe. For the psychoanalyst, the capacity for awe is as important as the capacity for humility. Our fast-paced technological culture does not generally foster the experience of awe. In fact, contemporary "civilization" tends to obliterate the sense of awe. From light pollution, that practically obliterates the majestic night sky, to the focus on materialistic comforts and modern technologies that tend to keep us more and more insulated from the natural world and from ourselves as well as from a fuller sense of aliveness, the experience of awe can be a rare occurrence in today's world. Reading about quantum physics has fostered in me a sense of wonder. I now observe the vastness of the night sky or the vastness of the human mind with a different inner sensibility.

Gargiulo (2016) writes:

> Mystery, not formula, guides our interactions with the world, with each other and with one's patients. By mystery I mean an ever-inviting horizon to our knowledge that beckons us. One must walk cautiously, knowing that what one knows is mostly the unknown; quantum physics models help in the appreciation of the great unknown.
>
> (p. 78)

Mystery, awe and a sense of wonder lead to an enhanced feeling of aliveness, which for me has made for an increased sense of aliveness in the consulting room. From an existential or phenomenological perspective, the experience of awe helps to lessen one's inner constriction, expand one's limited horizons and deepen one's subjective or phenomenological experience of aliveness. This can only benefit the analyst in his or her work with patients, who often come to us as a result of severe constrictions in being. The ultimate objective, after all, in most analyses is to foster an increased experience of aliveness.

Conclusion

Freud's universe was infinitesimally smaller as compared to our universe today in that, prior to the astronomer Edwin Hubble, there was no knowledge of the billions of galaxies comprising the cosmos or any knowledge that our universe is expanding. Freud lived in a different universe than we do today, a vastly smaller universe dominated by Newtonian physics. And his metaphors for the mind came from Newtonian physics.

As stated previously, the creation of new metaphors is crucial to keeping the psychoanalytic process vital and to keeping psychoanalysis alive. From the time of Freud, with his hydraulic model of the mind based on the metaphor of the steam engine, science has always provided metaphors for our work. Quantum physics, for me at least, offers new and revitalizing metaphors for our clinical work.

Journeying into the world of quantum mechanics has helped me to foster what I am calling a quantum sensibility. In summary, the following factors are what I see as comprising a quantum sensibility:

- The inseparability between observer and observed and between subject and object.
- A sense of there being no ultimate truth – only "a mist of infinite possibilities."
- Movement from a predictable and deterministic universe to one of indeterminacy, randomness and probability.
- An antireductionist sensibility – awareness of the profound level of interconnectedness and holism underlying the cosmos and all its interactions, including human interaction.
- A sense of humility, awe and aliveness that inevitably comes into being when confronting the mysteries surrounding us and when confronting our place in the cosmos.

References

Augustine, St. (1943). *The Confessions of St. Augustine* (J. G. Pilkington, Trans.). New York: Liveright Publishing Corporation.
Barad, K. M. (2007). *Meeting the Universe Halfway: Quantum Physics and the Entanglement of Matter and Meaning.* Durham, NC: Duke University Press.
Barrett, W. (1979). *The Illusion of Technique: A Search for Meaning in a Technological Civilization.* New York: Anchor Press/Doubleday.

Bohm, D. (1980). *Wholeness and the Implicate Order*. London and New York: Routledge.

Bromberg, P. M. (1993). Shadow and substance: A relational perspective on clinical process. *Psychoanalytic Psychology*, 10, 147–168.

Carroll, S. (2019). *Something Deeply Hidden: Quantum Worlds and the Emergence of Spacetime*. New York: Dutton.

Coburn, W. J. (2014). *Psychoanalytic Complexity: Clinical Attitudes for Therapeutic Change*. London and New York: Routledge.

d'Espagnat, B. (2006). *On Physics and Philosophy*. Princeton, NJ: Princeton University Press.

Einstein, A. (1930). What I believe. *Forum and Century*, 84, 193–194; AEA 78–645.

Frie, R. (1997). *Subjectivity and Intersubjectivity in Modern Philosophy: A Study of Sartre, Binswanger, Lacan, and Habermas*. New York: Rowman & Littlefield Publishers, Inc.

———. (2002). Modernism or postmodernism? Binswanger, Sullivan, and the problem of agency in contemporary psychoanalysis. *Contemporary Psychoanalysis*, 38, 635–673.

———. (Ed.). (2003). *Understanding Experience: Psychotherapy and Postmodernism*. London and New York: Routledge.

Fromm, E. (1947). *Man for Himself: An Inquiry into the Psychology of Ethics*. New York: Henry Holt and Company. New York: Simon and Schuster.

Gargiulo, G. J. (2016). *Quantum Psychoanalysis: Essays on Physics, Mind, and Analysis Today*. New York: International Psychoanalytic Books.

Grandy, D. A. (2009). *The Speed of Light: Constancy and Cosmos*. Bloomington, IN: Indiana University Press.

Hirsch, I. (1994). Dissociation and the interpersonal self. *Contemporary Psychoanalysis*, 30, 777–799.

Howell, E. F. (2011). *Understanding and Treating Dissociative Identity Disorder: A Relational Approach*. London and New York: Routledge.

Krauss, L. (2017). *The Greatest Story Ever Told – So Far: Why Are We Here?* New York: Atria Books.

Lakoff, G. and Johnson, M. (1980). *Metaphors We Live By*. Chicago: The University of Chicago Press.

Levenson, E. A. (1981). Facts or fantasies: – On the nature of psychoanalytic data. *Contemporary Psychoanalysis*, 17, 486–500.

———. (1996). A monopedal presentation of interpersonal psychoanalysis. *The Review of Interpersonal Psychoanalysis, William Alanson White Institute of Psychiatry, Psychoanalysis and Psychology,* 1(1), 1–4.

May, R., Angel, E. & Ellenberger, H. F. (Eds.). (1958). *Existence: A New Dimension in Psychiatry and Psychology*. New York: Simon and Schuster.

Orzel, C. (2019). Many worlds, but too much metaphor. *Forbes*. Retrieved from www.forbes.com/sites/chadorzel/2019/09/17/many-worlds-but-too-much-metaphor/#615bf203625d

Rosenblum, B. & Kuttner, F. (2011). *Quantum Enigma: Physics Encounters Consciousness*. New York: Oxford University Press.

Rovelli, C. (2021). *Helgoland: Making Sense of the Quantum Revolution* (E. Segre and S. Carnell, Trans.). New York: Riverhead Books. (Original work published in 2020).

Spurgeon, C. H. (1922). In Roberts, K. L. *Hoyt's New Cyclopedia of Practical Quotations*. New York: Funk & Wagnalls Company.

Stern, D. B. (1997). *Unformulated Experience: From Dissociation to Imagination in Psychoanalysis*. London and New York: Routledge.

Stolorow, R. D., Atwood, G. E. & Orange, D. M. (2002). *Worlds of Experience: Interweaving Philosophical and Clinical Dimensions in Psychoanalysis*. New York: Basic Books.

Part 2

Nonlinear Dynamic Systems Theory and Psychoanalysis

Chapter 3

Chaos and Complexity Theory
New Metaphors and Models for Psychoanalysis

John Turtz, PhD

"Chaos often breeds life, when order breeds habit."

Henry Adams (1907)

"In all chaos there is a cosmos, in all disorder a secret order."

Carl G. Jung (1969)

What does the study of nonlinear dynamic systems, through the lenses of chaos and complexity theory, have to do with psychoanalysis? The significance of this scientific field for psychoanalysis lies in the realization that the relationship between the analyst and analysand is in and of itself a nonlinear dynamic system. The purpose of this chapter is to introduce the reader to significant concepts from chaos and complexity theory and to demonstrate their potential usefulness and value to clinical practice. After giving a brief historical introduction to chaos theory, I will elaborate on what differentiates linear dynamic systems from nonlinear dynamic systems. Following this, I will define chaos theory and complexity theory and then explore concepts from these nonlinear dynamic theories that pertain to psychoanalytic work, including fractals, strange attractors, the butterfly effect, holism, emergence and self-organization. I will conclude by reflecting upon the concepts and metaphors that we can take from chaos and complexity theory and use to enhance the psychoanalytic process with our patients in the clinical consulting room.

When you enter the world of chaos and complexity theory, you enter the magical world of fractals and strange attractors. It is a world replete with mystery and enchantment. And the world of chaos and complexity theory is the world in which the psychoanalytic relationship between analyst and analysand plays out in the consulting room every day.

DOI: 10.4324/9781003271499-6

The science writer James Gleick, in his tour de force on chaos theory, wrote:

> The most passionate advocates for the new science go so far as to say that twentieth-century science will be remembered for just three things: relativity, quantum mechanics, and chaos. Chaos, they contend, has become the century's third great revolution in the physical sciences. Like the first two revolutions, chaos cuts away at the tenets of Newton's physics. Relativity eliminated the Newtonian illusion of absolute space and time; quantum theory eliminated the Newtonian dream of a controllable measurement process; and chaos eliminates the fantasy of deterministic predictability. Of the three, the revolution in chaos applies to the universe we see and touch, to objects at human scale.
>
> (Gleick, 1987, pp. 5–6)

Chaos and complexity theory investigate nonlinear dynamic systems. Whereas linear dynamic systems represent proportional relationships between input into the system and output, nonlinear dynamic systems are systems that change over time in a nonproportional manner – the relationship of input into the system to output is not proportional. These systems contain variables that generate disorder. Newton's Laws of Motion, for example, do not deal with the problematic variables of air and friction and therefore apply to linear dynamic systems. If we take air and friction into account, we then encounter disorder and thereby move into the world of nonlinear dynamics. The outcome of a nonlinear dynamic system is very dependent upon the system's initial conditions, and very slight differences in the initial conditions lead to tremendous differences in the evolution and outcome of the system.

The French mathematician Henri Poincaré was the first to discover what is referred to as *sensitive dependence on initial conditions* in the later part of the 19th century in his work on what is known in physics as the three-body problem. He revealed that a small difference in initial conditions may lead to a large difference in outcome, thus eliminating the possibility of accurate prediction of the motions of three celestial bodies. He thereby discovered deterministic chaos – a nonlinear dynamic system that, because of sensitive dependence on initial conditions, is unpredictable yet still deterministic. Though the term *chaos theory* had not yet come into existence, Poincaré had discovered the underpinnings of chaos theory.

Sensitive dependence on initial conditions was rediscovered by the meteorologist Edward Lorenz in 1961 in his computer analyses of simulated weather predictions. Exceedingly small differences in the initial conditions programmed into the computer led to major differences in the outcome of these weather predictions. The mathematician James Yorke gave chaos theory its name in the 1970s, and the birth of this new science ensued.

I believe it is important for psychoanalysts to look beyond the narrow confines of formal psychoanalytic theory to other fields and disciplines in order to broaden, expand and enrich psychoanalysis and maintain its vitality and aliveness. Chaos and complexity theory are two such interrelated fields that can greatly enrich the field of psychoanalysis.

Dynamical Systems

In simplest terms, dynamical systems are systems that evolve and change over time. One investigates variables as they change over time, as seen through the phase space (also called state space) of a system, a set of points where each point represents the complete state of the system at that particular moment in time. Dynamical systems are described by differential equations. Differential equations for linear dynamic systems are relatively easy to solve. For example, differential equations that solve for the future motion of two celestial bodies (when their initial positions and velocities are known) involve simple linear dynamics, which is why Newtonian physics can be used to fly a rocket ship to the moon and back. However, solvable differential equations for two-body problems become unsolvable when a third body is brought into the system – the *three-body problem* arises in physics when you add a third celestial body to the system. Now you enter the world of nonlinear dynamics, where there is great sensitivity to the initial conditions of the positions and velocities of the celestial bodies. Chaos theory and complexity theory both investigate nonlinear dynamic systems.

Nonlinear dynamic systems include variables that generate disorder and complexity. Prior to the revolution of chaos theory, scientists attempted to eliminate or at least reduce the impact of these variables. Chaos theory, in contrast, directly focuses on these variables. "The genius of Chaos theory was to invert the order of interest and to focus on the disorder, rather than considering it as simply an interference with the prevailing orderly development" (Levenson, 1994, p. 18). Due to the complex nature of disorder, the thorny study of chaotic systems (from turbulence to weather to heart rhythms) could only take off and blossom after the advent of computer technology.

Chaos theory investigates nonlinear dynamic systems that consist of very few variables. These chaotic systems are extremely sensitive to initial conditions. Complexity theory studies nonlinear dynamic systems that comprise more elements than do chaotic systems. Complexity theory investigates complex adaptive systems, systems which exhibit two important features: emergence and self-organization. Both chaotic systems and complex systems are impossible to predict, but chaotic systems are deterministic whereas complex systems are nondeterministic.

The reason that nonlinear dynamical systems are important to psychoanalysis is that, as previously stated, the relationship between an analyst and analysand is itself a nonlinear dynamic system, a system that can move toward what is termed the *edge of chaos* (when the system becomes more and more disorderly, but does not enter a state of complete disorder), where small inputs into the system can create large impacts upon outcome and where fractals and strange attractors appear. The nonlinear dynamical relationship between analyst and analysand also forms a complex adaptive system, where emergence, self-organization and adaptation can transpire. I will now proceed to further explore and examine these concepts and their application and usefulness to psychoanalysis.

What Exactly Is Chaos?

In a technical sense, the term *chaos* refers to those systems that are extremely sensitive to initial conditions, systems that are unpredictable yet deterministic. One can never measure the initial conditions precisely enough to be able to predict outcomes because an extremely small difference in input can lead to a huge difference in output. A wonderful example of chaos in the real world is that of weather, and it is the sensitive dependence on initial conditions that makes accurate weather prediction impossible beyond a relatively short period of time. Chaos theory is the study of these chaotic systems, systems that appear to be disordered yet ultimately reveal hidden patterns.

Fractals

Chaos theory has discovered that underlying what appears to be randomness and apparent chaos is a hidden order, which emerges over time. This order is of a fractal design. Imagine a computer that generates random numbers, and each number corresponds to a specific position marked by a point on the computer screen. As the computer generates random numbers, most people would expect to see random points appear on the screen. But if the program runs long enough, one begins to see emerging patterns. And these patterns have the following characteristic: as one moves from the pattern as a whole to smaller and smaller sections of the whole pattern, one sees that the pattern replicates itself at all scales (though with some loss of detail moving from larger to smaller sections). This is called a fractal design and has been compared to Russian nesting dolls.

When you become aware of fractals, you begin to see them everywhere. The next time you look at a large tree, notice how the trunk may branch in two. And then notice how each branch of the tree then also branches in two and so on, from the largest to the smallest of branches. And fractal-like patterns occur in psychoanalytic treatment, which is why one small segment of a session may demonstrate the same pattern as the session as a whole.

Fractal designs (also referred to as self-similarity) are an apt metaphor for the patterns that occur between analyst and analysand. I do want to highlight that we are talking about a metaphor here and therefore need to be very careful not to reify these metaphors. Fractals in nature are in fact different from the "fractals" that emerge in psychoanalysis. Daniel Stern (2004) actually pointed to this very issue in his book *The Present Moment in Psychotherapy and Everyday Life*. A true fractal formed in nature is based on each successive present moment – the immediate local conditions – whereas in psychoanalysis, we are always dealing with the silent psychodynamic past and implicit relational knowing. But Stern (2004) also writes: "In short, as far as the 'silent past' is concerned, the difference between fractals and psychodynamic instantiations is only theoretical and not phenomenological" (p. 205).

Imagine a patient who begins a session complaining about the weather, saying, "It's so cold out there this morning." He then moves into how his wife is not supporting him around an issue with their child. From there, he moves into how the therapist does not appear to be very understanding or supportive around the issues he is having with his wife. This would be an example of a fractal – the underlying pattern that plays out over and over again on different scales is this individual's feeling of being alone and unsupported in a cold, uncaring world.

I work with a young woman in her 20s who illustrates a fractal pattern in her way of being in and moving through the world. I will call her Allison. Allison, currently a graduate student, can only view herself through a negative lens. She does not see herself as smart, competent or attractive. She assumes people will not like her before she even meets them. She assumes that everyone in her class is smarter than her. She assumes that she will never be able to be in an intimate relationship, or at best, that the only kind of guy she could possibly have a relationship with would be someone with major emotional problems. And she experiences each of her assumptions as a fact of life, as opposed to suppositions that she herself has constructed.

Allison views her underlying assumptions about herself and the world as absolute truth. I see her underlying assumptions as the building blocks of her generalized mode of relating to the world, which is to avoid entering and engaging with the world as much as possible. Others are not to be trusted. She is not to enter their world, and she is not to allow others into her isolated world. From her relationships with peers to family to me, she has great difficulty letting people into her world. She learned early on from real experience that letting others in leads to danger.

From the smallest to the largest scale, from the least significant to the most profound of issues, Allison's pattern is to avoid connection and isolate herself from the world. She does this by seeing the world and herself through a lens of negativity. She speaks about having little hope for the future. She feels she will never find a boyfriend. She worries about whether she will graduate from her current program and doesn't think she will ever be able to land a job (and if she were inexplicably able to find employment, her boss would not like her anyway). From the most minor to the most major issues in her life, the pattern is the same – she will not engage with and enter the world of others. And she will not let others enter her isolated and solitary cocoon. And on top of all this, she eradicates her future. By eliminating an imagined future, she is able to hold onto an illusion that she will be able to avoid being hurt. I believe this is the type of individual that the existential analyst Rollo May is referring to when he wrote:

> The existential therapists also observed that the most profound psychological experiences are peculiarly those which shake the individual's relation to time. Severe anxiety and depression blot out time, annihilate the future. Or, as Minkowski proposes, it may be that the disturbance of the patient in relation to time, his inability to "have" a future, gives rise to his anxiety and depression. In either case, the most painful aspect of the sufferer's predicament is that he is unable to imagine a future moment in time when he will be out of the anxiety or depression. We see a similar close interrelationship between the disturbance of the time function and neurotic symptoms.
>
> (May et al., 1958, p. 68)

Most sessions begin with how terrible her life is and how nothing has much changed. She then focuses on the specifics – how she hates school, how she feels very isolated and alone (especially during the current pandemic) and how her life "sucks" in every which way. If I in any way question one of her underlying assumptions, she stubbornly finds a way to counteract what I say and thereby keep me at bay. From the smallest to the largest scale, she finds a way to maintain distance from others and to negate hope and any sense of a future. Whatever the issue, she displays mistrust of and contempt toward others and herself and eliminates the potential for a future. This is the fractal pattern – keeping others at a distance in order to prevent the possibility of connection leading to future hurt and loss. No matter what the content under discussion is, the process reveals a reiterative pattern – one of negating herself, the world and the future.

In one last example of the fractal quality of an individual's behavior in the consulting room, an example I referred to in a previous paper (Turtz, 2020), a patient in his 50s early in treatment began a session by asking me how therapy works and by letting me know in no uncertain terms that he would like me to provide him with a roadmap. The exploration of this desire revealed a fear of the unknown. For this individual, entering uncharted waters resulted in the dangerous possibility of connecting with feelings of intolerable sadness. By exploring the desire for a roadmap, we saw how his search for external rules in many areas of his life (from the smallest to the largest of problems) was a way for him to disavow intolerable feelings of sadness that he carried within.

Attractors

In chaos theory, attractors are the values that dynamical systems and their variables evolve toward. Strange attractors are attractors that have a fractal quality to them and that are highly dependent on initial conditions. Strange attractors, as with fractals, illustrate the hidden order underlying a chaotic system. As the psychoanalyst Galatzer-Levy (2017) wrote, "Upon first examination, the motions in systems may seem random and disorganized, but after many repetitions, we can see that they tend toward a particular pattern – not in the sense that they settle down but rather that the apparently wild shifts in the motion represent tendencies to complex but representable patterns."

To further understand the concept of strange attractors, one needs to examine phase space, the graphic representation of a process whereby each point represents the state of the system at that particular moment in time. As the state of a system evolves, what at first appears in phase space to be senseless movement, over time begins to reveal a pattern that emerges from the apparent chaos. The movements, as seen in phase space, never repeat in exactly the same way, but the points do tend toward what are termed *basins of attraction*. Here you have an infinity of different ways of approaching the basins of attraction within a finite space. The famous Lorenz attractor has two basins of attraction and takes the form of a butterfly, which is where the butterfly effect got its name. The paths from one basin to the other are never exactly the same, and the precise moment at which the system shifts and moves from one basin toward the other is unpredictable.

There are other types of attractors as well, such as fixed point attractors, which describe systems that evolve toward a single point or basin of attraction, and periodic attractors, which describe attractors that evolve toward two or more points and periodically move from one basin of attraction to another. Attractors are a concept that can help the clinician to think about and assess a patient's level of emotional well-being. Galatzer-Levy (2017) has written about the concept of attractors and how they can be used with regard to thinking about psychopathology. From a nonlinear dynamics perspective, psychopathology can be viewed as the degree of organization or disorganization with regard to movement toward basins of attraction. More specifically, either too much organization (rigid adherence to basins of attraction) or too much disorganization (lack of any organized pattern of movement toward basins of attraction) can indicate psychopathology. Galatzer-Levy (2017) writes, "Psychological health involves engaging attractors that are neither too rigid nor too disorganized. These attractors are sufficiently complex that rich creative possibilities exist in them" (p. 104). Given this thinking, one can more easily see the value of working at the edge of chaos.

Basins of attraction are an apt metaphor for the different self-states and interpersonal patterns that individuals are drawn to. Abrupt and unpredictable change can occur as self-states move toward different basins of attraction. I work with a man who tends to be drawn toward two very different self-states (what I would consider to be a periodic attractor). In one self-state, he is congenial, warm and humorous. In the other, he tightens up dramatically and takes on an angry and intimidating countenance. There is no precise way of predicting when these changes will occur, but these are two core self-states that the patient repeatedly moves toward in his relationships with others. These two self-states are analogous to basins of attraction; he gets drawn into these self-states, but the moment of change cannot be precisely predicted and can also be quite abrupt.

Let me return to my work with Allison in order to further illustrate the concept of fixed point attractors and the crucial importance of working at the edge of chaos. Fixed point attractors, which describe systems that evolve toward a single point, are not strange attractors, but can also illustrate the importance of working at the edge of chaos. From the perspective of fixed point attractors, Allison can be seen as a woman that rigidly adheres to a self-state that has become a major part of the way she moves through her world. This self-state can be viewed as her singular basin of attraction. She lives in the past, a past filled with regret, disappointment and self-blame, and she cannot access a future. I see these ways of relating to the world as reflections of her core self-state – a self-state that entails dread of the world of others along with self-contempt, self-blame and shame. This woman is very frightened of engagement – engaging with others, engaging with the world and engaging with life. Her core self-state not only keeps her in her self-protective and isolated bubble or cocoon; this self-state is the very fabric and structure of the cocoon itself. From the perspective of attractors, this cocoon is her very rigid basin of attraction.

Deconstruction, disorder and movement toward the edge of chaos are exactly what is needed for the potential transformation of my patient's rigid pattern of movement toward this singular basin of attraction. The edge of chaos, as previously noted, is a state somewhere between rigid order and chaotic disorganization, where novelty and surprise can emerge. An example whereby I tried to shake up Allison's very tightly ordered system occurred during a session in which she focused upon her pessi-mistic expectations of not being able to find a job after completing her graduate studies. Graduation was still a few years away, and I asked her to elaborate on what was making her so anxious at this moment in time. She spoke of her despair around being able to find a job, stating she feels she has nothing to offer. At the same time, she stressed the crucial impor-tance of becoming fully self-sufficient in the future, a direct result of her assumption that she would never be in a relationship and would conse-quently have to take total care of herself. Her focus was on her obsessive drivenness toward self-sufficiency as well as her sense of hopelessness about ever attaining this. I attempted to shake up and deconstruct her underlying framework and the assumptions that formed its foundation (assumptions which, as stated earlier, she experienced as fact). From a nonlinear dynamic systems perspective, I was attempting to add disorder to what I felt was a rigid adherence to one particular basin of attraction. I therefore said something to the effect of, "Your goal in life appears to be self-sufficiency. You seem to see self-sufficiency as the answer to your problems. And from your worldview, you define self-sufficiency as a criti-cal aspect of mental health. I, on the other hand, see the problem as being your difficulty in tolerating interdependency and engaged interaction with others. From my perspective, your difficulty stems from your anxieties about connecting with others, not from your inability to achieve some form of self-sufficiency." From the vantage point of chaos and complexity theory, I was trying to move this patient from a position of strict adherence to a single rigid basin of attraction more toward the edge of chaos, where divergent thinking and creative change have more potential for emerg-ing. I certainly do not want to imply that this one intervention resolved this issue, as a lot of repetition tends to be required in our profession, but Allison did appear to be very intrigued by my deconstructive efforts. And she exhibited a noticeably more open, self-reflective and curious attitude in this particular clinical session.

I will add that the perspective of nonlinear dynamics can facilitate hope in the therapist, even with patients that rigidly adhere to certain basins of attraction. This is because from a nonlinear dynamics perspective, the possibility of abrupt change is always present, and when this change actually occurs cannot be predicted. The system defines its own terms for change through its own unique patterns of interaction. Knowing that change can be abrupt and unpredictable can help the therapist to maintain hope and persevere through the toughest of times with a patient.

From a more Kleinian perspective, another example of attractors would be the patient that continually moves back and forth between the paranoid-schizoid position and the depressive position. One cannot precisely predict when moments of change will occur, but with this kind of individual, the basins of attraction draw the person back and forth between these two Kleinian positions.

One can also see how attractors play out between partners in couples treatment that integrates psychoanalytic theory with systems theory. Take a couple that is drawn to fighting (I know it's hard to imagine!). Whatever the topic, whatever the surface issue, the couple is drawn to fighting like a moth to a flame. Some couples are so adept at this that a warm statement from one to the other can turn on a dime when the partner receiving the warm statement metaphorically takes in the warm milk, sours it and spits it back out at his or her partner. A strong basin of attraction for this couple is the draw to turning any interaction into a fight, a power struggle over control, dominance and autonomy. Treatment would consist of moving from this rigid basin of attraction toward the edge of chaos, where a novel way of interacting can then emerge.

Butterfly Effect

The term butterfly effect stems from the idea that the flapping of a butterfly's wings in Asia could theoretically cause a hurricane in the Caribbean a few weeks later. In other words, a very small input can lead to a very large difference in output in a system.

In psychoanalysis, I think the butterfly effect is a wonderful metaphor for how seemingly small moments in treatment can lead to large impacts. Often these moments can come in the form of implicit relational knowing (Stern, 2004). I once asked a patient very early in treatment if his spouse ever apologized to him. What seemed like a relatively straightforward and not particularly profound question became a symbol for this individual of my adeptness at listening to him and understanding his world, a moment he kept returning to in treatment. Who knows? If I had not asked this question, perhaps he may not have formed such a positive therapeutic alliance and may not have remained in treatment for as long as he has. Another patient stated he was greatly impacted by my rather simple statement that he might try to stay more in the moment with his kids. In truth, I'm not even sure I recall having made this statement! As Levenson (1994) wrote:

> For an engagingly trivial instance of our "butterfly effect", I've always been astonished by how wonderfully helpful patients often find totally banal remarks from the therapist; as, "I never promised you a rose garden", or, "Rome wasn't built in a day". One hears these funny reports from therapists who ask a patient, after nine years of treatment, what was it that seemed to make the difference and are told that, "Well, about three years into the treatment you said, 'Don't wish your life away'". What ever became of all the painfully elaborated wonderful insights?
>
> (p. 19)

Holism

Chaos and complexity theory are anti-reductionist. Put most simply, this means that the whole is more than the sum of its parts. One cannot understand a system simply by reducing it to smaller and smaller parts and then investigating and analyzing these elements. Chaos and complexity theory are holistic – they focus on the manner in which the elements of a system interact with each other and the manner in which these interactions generate something novel that is greater than the sum of its parts. From general systems theory to quantum physics to chaos and complexity theory, holism has become the new paradigm in much of contemporary science. As mentioned in Chapter 2, the physicist David Bohm beautifully depicted this when he wrote, "Ultimately, the entire universe (with all its 'particles,' including those constituting human beings, their laboratories, observing instruments, etc.) has to be understood as a single undivided whole, in which analysis into separately and independently existent parts has no fundamental status" (as cited in Grandy, 2009, p. 73). The naturalist John

Muir put this even more poetically when he wrote, "When we try to pick out anything by itself, we find it hitched to everything else in the Universe" (Muir, 1911, 1988, p. 110).

Each analyst and analysand pair form a unique dyad, and this dyad is always more than the sum of each individual part. If you could somehow conceivably know everything about each individual in the therapist-patient system, you would not be able to predict what would emerge from their patterns of interaction. Chaos and complexity theory provide support for the significance of holism as contrasted with reductionism. And from this perspective, the system creates its own agent of change, and change itself cannot be predicted. The agent of change emerges out of the relational patterns of interaction that comprise the system itself. We have left the reductionistic domain of the linear Newtonian cause-effect framework of thought.

With regard to pathology, a therapist drawn to holism tends to broaden the site of pathology from within the individual to the individual in context. The individual is always seen in relationship and inextricably embedded in context. As Gargiulo (2004) wrote, "Human beings do not have relationships; they are relationships. No meaningful analytic work can be done without that awareness" (p. 98). And Stolorow and Atwood (2019), from a phenomenological perspective, have demonstrated the importance of moving from the isolated mind of Cartesian thinking toward "Heidegger's ontological contextualism" (p. 16). From Heidegger's perspective, the essence of being for human beings is *Being-in-the-world*. We are never separate from the world; we are never separate from context. Chaos and complexity theory focus on relationships and demonstrate how, in the context of complex interactions between two or more individuals, something new and creative can emerge.

Emergence and Self-Organization

As stated previously, complex adaptive systems exhibit two features beyond those of self-similarity and the capacity to learn and adapt. These two features are emergence and self-organization. Emergence is the process by which complexity develops in a nonhierarchical manner through local interactions among elements of a system, that becomes self-organizing by way of the patterns of interaction and feedback loops occurring among its elements. This is *not* top-down functioning, as in the chain of command in a corporate structure or in the military. There is no executive making decisions from the top. All decisions result from simple rules that apply at the local level.

The example of emergence that I most appreciate is that of harvester ants. Steven Johnson (2001), in his book *Emergence*, discusses how harvester ants, by following simple rules at the local level, create a complex adaptive system (a system that demonstrates emergence). These ants build a cemetery (yes, an actual place where they put their dead) that is as far away as possible from the ant colony. And they also build what is called a midden, a place where waste products are brought. What is most remarkable is that the ants build the midden as far away as possible from both the cemetery and the colony. As the behavioral ecologist Deborah Gordon put it, "It's like there's a rule they're following: put the dead ants as far away as possible, and put the midden as far away as possible without putting it near the dead ants" (Gordon, as cited in Johnson, 2001, p. 33). How can ants (each one lacking great intelligence) generate a collective intelligence such as this and all without any particular ant in charge? Well, it's all done by following local rules, that is, rules followed by each individual ant given its current location. In the case of harvester ants, the local rules are governed by chemical pheromones. So, what you have here is a collective intelligence that emerges from a system of unintelligent elements with no organizational, top-down structure. All this occurs through bottom-up processes at the local level. As Johnson (2001) writes, "The movement from low-level rules to higher-level sophistication is what we call emergence" (p. 18).

Bottom-up approaches in the psychoanalytic process refer to those nonconscious, implicit aspects of interaction that form somatic experience. They are nonconscious and therefore outside our awareness, but they are not unconscious in the psychodynamic sense, whereby conscious experience, which is capable of being formulated, is so toxic and unacceptable that it needs to be repressed. The focus of bottom-up approaches is on the recognition of and deepening of experience as opposed to the cognitive understanding and interpretation of experience.

As Stern (2004) has pointed out, much of what plays out between analyst and analysand occurs at the implicit level. This is the level of facial expressions, body language and all that is occurring that we cannot be conscious of (not because it is unacceptable as in the traditional Freudian

dynamic unconscious, but because there is simply too much information coming at us for us to be fully conscious of, and because much of
this information is nonverbal and unable to be formulated in language).
Donnel Stern (1997) termed this *unformulated experience*. When considering bottom-up approaches, it is helpful to view what is occurring
between analyst and analysand through the lens of a dissociative model of
unconscious processes as opposed to a repression model. We are talking
about experience that has never been formulated, but that has been unwit-
tingly internalized nonetheless through repeated patterns of interaction
and then lived out in mutual enactment with the therapist (Hirsch, 1994;
Hirsch and Roth, 1995).

The capacity to tolerate not knowing and not understanding what is
occurring between the analyst and analysand is crucial to the psychoanalytic process because the analyst cannot force the hidden patterns to emerge
through some kind of forced interaction. The analyst must be patient and
tolerate a lack of understanding for a long enough period of time to allow
the hidden patterns to emerge and be visible. It can be a rather astonish-
ing experience to tolerate not knowing long enough for these patterns to
emerge in the space between therapist and patient. The singer-songwriter
Arlo Guthrie said, "Songwriting is like fishing in a stream; you put in
your line and hope to catch something. And I don't think anyone down-
stream from Bob Dylan ever caught anything." Though I love the tribute to
Dylan, I bring up this quotation to highlight the creative process and how
it is like casting out a fishing line and hoping that something emerges. The
quality of emergence is such that it feels like it is generated somewhere
outside of oneself. Think of the inspiration that comes to an artist. The
word "inspire" has Latin roots, meaning "to breathe or blow into." Inspiration is the breath; metaphorically, it is what is breathed into the space
between the world and the individual, and in the case of psychoanalysis,
between the therapist and patient. It does not emerge from inside one individual; it emerges in the in-between space, similar to Winnicott's views on
transitional phenomena.

Emergence was of critical importance in the treatment of a man I once
worked with. For a long period of time, I had to tolerate a good deal of
uncertainty and not knowing. He was very open when discussing his issues,
but I often had a feeling that I was missing something. What emerged in the
space between us was that he could be verbally open and transparent about

his needs and his flaws, but what he could not do was in any way burden others with his needs and vulnerabilities. He grew up in a chaotic family system and had to learn to rely on himself in order to survive. He simply could not rely on his rather disorganized mother, and his father was absent. What emerged in treatment was how he did the same thing with me – he could talk *about* his issues, but he could not be vulnerable enough to connect with his emotional experience around these issues in my presence. Over time, the capacity to connect with emotional experience emerged and developed in the therapeutic space. This emerged because of many complex interacting variables, including variables at the level of "implicit relational knowing" (Stern, 2004). The point here is not to go into exactly how this process occurred (as if one could precisely pinpoint this process in the first place), but to demonstrate the importance of following the flow of the treatment and tolerating uncertainty long enough for something new to emerge as opposed to trying to force something new to develop. In other words, one has to tolerate not knowing and not understanding long enough to allow the mysteries of the psychoanalytic process to play out in such a way that emergence of something new can occur in the space between analyst and analysand; attempting to force meaning and understanding in a top-down manner does not allow for the bottom-up, implicit processes to emerge, and these bottom-up, implicit processes are essential to creativity and to the nature of healing. As Stern (2004) writes, "With an emphasis on implicit experience rather than explicit content, therapeutic aims shift more to the deepening and enriching of experience and less to the under-standing of meaning" (p. 222).

Let me add just a bit more complexity to complexity theory! "Coupled systems of oscillators are rich in emergent phenomena that can result from them" (Galatzer-Levy, 2017, p. 112). An oscillator is something that repeats a pattern. A swinging pendulum is an example of an oscil-lator. Coupled oscillators occur when two oscillators become connected. A famous example is that of the syncing of two pendulums when they are in the same room together. They may begin their movements out of sync, but the two pendulums' back and forth motion becomes synced over time. As previously stated, coupled oscillators tend to generate emergence. This is significant because each analyst-analysand pair tends to become a system of coupled oscillators. "In the analytic situation, two oscillators, the mind-brains of analysand and analyst, are coupled by producing a new oscillator, the analytic dyad. This new oscillator is of a higher dimension than either of the oscillators separately so that new solutions to previously unsolvable problems may emerge" (Galatzer-Levy, 2017, pp. 114–115). Galatzer-Levy (2017) goes on to write, "Much of the apparent work of analysis involves creating a setup in which mutual influence can occur. In this model, interpretation and insight *per se* would play a much smaller role in analysis than they do in older formulations. They are no longer the centerpiece of the analytic process" (p. 116). Stern (2004), through his work with the Boston Change Process Study Group, has demonstrated the importance of implicit modes of relating that heal by way of bottom-up processes. One way in which to better understand these implicit ways of relating and how they can lead to the emergence of something new and creative between the analyst and the analysand is through the lens of seeing this relationship as a coupled oscillator.

Conclusion: Metaphors and Concepts From Chaos and Complexity Theory and Their Application to Psychoanalysis

What are the metaphors and concepts that we can take from chaos and complexity theory and use to enrich the psychoanalytic process? I find that the metaphors of fractals and strange attractors, as long as they are not reified, are extremely useful and applicable to the psychoanalytic process. As Levenson (1994) highlighted, the therapy process can be seen as a deconstructive process, that is, a process of deconstructing the patient's narrative by searching for gaps and omissions in the story, thereby leading the patient to use self-protective mechanisms that he or she has always used. However, this time these self-protective mechanisms are enacted with the analyst in the transference-countertransference matrix. If the analyst can tolerate not knowing and avoid trying to force understanding, hidden patterns of interaction between the analyst and analysand will emerge and become more noticeable. These patterns, once enacted, can then be explored and examined. As with fractals, what the therapist may begin to notice is that these patterns of interaction, from the smallest and most ordinary of moments to the most meaningful, all reveal a self-similarity.

The basins of attraction found in attractors are a useful metaphor for the self-states and ways of moving through and relating to the world that a patient continually is drawn to. This metaphor is also a valuable reminder that change itself is unpredictable and can be abrupt. We tend to think of change as continuous and gradual and thereby tend to see abrupt change as somehow not genuine. Yet from the vantage point of chaos and complexity theory, real and substantial change can be quite abrupt. This can help the therapist to persevere and maintain hope when working with individuals drawn to very rigid patterns of moving through the world. Attractors and basins of attraction also provide new ways of thinking about psychological well-being and psychopathology, more in terms of levels of rigidity in one's patterns of moving through the world as opposed to DSM categorical diagnoses.

The butterfly effect is a superb metaphor for how small inputs or changes can have large ripple effects and thereby make huge impacts upon outcome. As Stern (2004) has pointed out, therapy is a sloppy process. If the therapist can allow him or herself to stay in the flow of this sloppy process, small inputs from the therapist may lead to greater change than the most magnificent of interpretations. Levenson (1994) writes:

> When improvement occurs in a patient, it may creep in almost before one notices it, or it may be sudden and dramatic. It may even take place after the therapy is over. But what impels the change, is never entirely clear to me; and it hardly ever seems to proceed in a clearcut fashion from something I've said or done. I do not mean to imply that I have done nothing or that, Heaven forbid, my patients do not improve. I am merely suggesting that the relationship between cause and effect is very complicated and that small efforts may produce immense changes and immense efforts, small or even negative effects. If the primary therapeutic activity is facilitating this flow, then too much understanding, too much effort at linear clarifying of the process, will block its appearance. If the process is rolling along, so to speak, with the therapist travelling on the crest of the wave; then, I suspect, small interventions – interpretive or enactments – may make a tremendous difference. It is a bit like trying to push a car with its brakes on and pushing one which is already rolling.
>
> (pp. 14–15)

Emergence is a metaphor for how what arises in the treatment always develops in the space between the analyst and analysand. What emerges from the self-organizing system made up of the interactions between the analyst and analysand is always inherently linked to the interpersonal field. With regard to the nature and process of change itself, emergence demonstrates how "change is generated by the vicissitudes of the self-organizing system itself, (i.e., its underlying patterns of interaction)" (Turtz, 2020, p. 179). Levenson (1994) puts it this way:

> Suffice it to say, that from this viewpoint, the process defines its own terms for change. In other words, one keeps expanding the field, and at some point it overloads and shifts. The nature and prerequisites for the shift are never entirely clear; but, as I said, small inputs can have major consequences.
>
> (1994, p. 19)

Coburn (2014) states that a therapist that is influenced by nonlinear dynamic systems theory must develop what he terms a *complexity sensibility*. Just some of the attitudes comprising a complexity sensibility, according to Coburn (2014), are as follows:

1 Awareness and respect for the complexity of the human condition.
2 Understanding that we are always embedded in contexts.
3 That we stay aware of the significance of history, current experience and the environment and the complex interactions among these aspects of experience.
4 The system creates its own agent of change.
5 Embracing what Coburn terms *epistemological ineptitude* – a tolerance for ambiguity and uncertainty and an awareness of our limitations.
6 *Radical hope*: "This type of hope may be realized given our understanding that complex systems are not rule-driven or predetermined but are quite literally open to change in ways that we may not yet be able to imagine" (Coburn, 2014, p. 12).

The core features of chaos and complexity theory that I bring to my work are as follows:

1 Following the sloppy or chaotic flow of the mysterious process that occurs between analyst and analysand allows for hidden patterns of interaction to appear, often fractal in nature; tolerating not knowing while following the flow is critical for these hidden patterns to emerge.

2   With regard to attractors, I find that the basins of attraction are useful in helping the therapist to be able to see that what may at first appear like abrupt and random changes may actually have a hidden order beneath the surface appearance. Attractors also provide a new vantage point for looking at emotional well-being and psychopathology.

3   The concept of emergence demonstrates the importance of bottom-up approaches, contextualism and implicit relational knowing in psychanalytic work.

4   The metaphor of working at the edge of chaos provides a wonderful objective to strive for – a dialectical tension between order and disorder that allows for novelty, creativity and transformation to emerge.

I once believed that the underlying philosophical principles of psychoanalysis and general systems theory were contradictory and incompatible. However, from an interpersonal/existential perspective, I no longer see these different systems of thought as incompatible. When one sees others as always in context and when one uses a dissociation model rather than repression model of unconscious processes, then holism becomes central to both psychoanalytic and systems thinking. As Edgar Levenson (1982) stated, "I would prefer to see the therapeutic leverage as lying in the resolution of a redundant interaction with a great deal of homeostatic power" (p. 11). Here you have a psychoanalyst speaking in the language of nonlinear dynamics systems theory.

I think it is crucial for analysts to look beyond psychoanalysis itself in order to broaden and enrich psychoanalysis. In contemporary science, nonlinear dynamic systems theory is one such field that can provide a model and framework that can help psychoanalysts to better understand the human condition and the mysteries of the psychoanalytic process.

References

Adams, H. (1907). The education of Henry Adams. *The Project Gutenberg EBook.* Retrieved from https://www.gutenberg.org/files/2044/2044-h/2044-h.htm

Coburn, W. J. (2014). *Psychoanalytic Complexity: Clinical Attitudes for Therapeutic Change.* London and New York: Routledge.

Galatzer-Levy, R. M. (2017). *Nonlinear Psychoanalysis: Notes from Forty Years of Chaos and Complexity Theory.* London and New York: Routledge.

Gargiulo, J. (2004). *Psyche, Self and Soul: Rethinking Psychoanalysis, the Self and Spirituality.* Philadelphia: Whurr Publishers.

Gleick, J. (1987). *Chaos: Making a New Science*. New York: Penguin Books.

Grandy, D. A. (2009). *The Speed of Light: Constancy and Cosmos*. Bloomington, IN: Indiana University Press.

Hirsch, I. (1994) Dissociation and the interpersonal self. *Contemporary Psychoanalysis*, 30, 777–799.

Hirsch, I. & Roth, J. (1995). Changing conceptions of unconscious. *Contemporary Psychoanalysis*, 31, 263–276.

Johnson, S. (2001). *Emergence: The Connected Lives of Ants, Brains, Cities, and Software*. New York: Scribner.

Jung, C. G. (1969). *The Archetypes and the Collective Unconscious*. Second edition. Princeton, NJ: Princeton University Press.

Levenson, E. (1982). Follow the fox – An inquiry into the vicissitudes of psychoanalytic supervision. Contemporary Psychoanalysis, 18, 1-15.

Levenson, E. (1994). The uses of disorder – Chaos theory and psychoanalysis. *Contemporary Psychoanalysis*, 30, 5–24.

May, R., Angel, E. & Ellenberger, H. F. (Eds.). (1958). *Existence: A New Dimension in Psychiatry and Psychology*. New York: Simon and Schuster.

Muir, J. (1911). *My First Summer in the Sierra*. San Francisco: Sierra Club Books. 1988.

Stern, D. B. (1997). *Unformulated Experience: From Dissociation to Imagination in Psychoanalysis*. London and New York: Routledge.

Stern, D. N. (2004). *The Present Moment in Psychotherapy and Everyday Life*. New York: W. W. Norton & Company.

Stolorow, R. D. & Atwood, G. E. (2019). *The Power of Phenomenology: Psychoanalytic and Philosophical Perspectives*. London and New York: Routledge.

Turtz, J. (2020). Mysteries of the psychoanalytic process: Reflections on chaos, complexity, and emergence. *The American Journal of Psychoanalysis*, 80, 176–195.

Chapter 4

Ecopsychoanalysis, Complexity and a Nonlinear Earth

Joseph Dodds, PhD

Complexity Theory as the Meta-Theory of Ecopsychoanalysis

Complexity theory is foundational to the field of *ecopsychoanalysis* (Dodds, 2011, 2012, 2013, 2019, 2020; Dodds and Poenaru, 2021), a transdisciplinary approach to thinking about the relationship between psychoanalysis, ecology, 'the natural' and the problem of climate change. Ecopsychoanalysis draws on a range of fields including psychoanalysis, psychology, ecology, philosophy, science, complexity theory, aesthetics and the humanities, with far reaching implications for psychoanalysis (clinical, theoretical and applied), challenging some basic premises of our discipline. This chapter seeks to demonstrate the centrality of complexity science to this endeavour.

First of all, complexity theory is required to understand the *nonlinear dynamics of a chaotic Earth*, its destabilisation points, attractors and complex feedback loops. Complexity science is necessary for any attempt to understand climate change and ecological processes. The Earth is a dynamic system with multiple levels, from atmospheric chemistry to carbon and water cycles, local and global ecosystems and food webs, and is in complex interaction with human societies and economies. Complexity theory gives an essential frame for integrating the various levels of ecological, biological and Earth science. At the same time, nonlinear dynamical systems provide new ways to think about nature more generally, and new approaches to 'intelligence' and 'mind', for example through the study of social insects, with radical implications for psychology and sociology. Complexity theory is also *just as essential* in understanding *psychological and social dynamics*. John Turtz's previous chapter illustrated the usefulness of this approach for psychoanalysis. In the following text I will expand these examples, and apply a similar approach for an

DOI: 10.4324/9781003271499-7

understanding of groups and social systems. As ecopsychoanalysis clearly demonstrates, psychoanalysis plays an important role well beyond its role in the consulting room.

Finally, as well as demonstrating that complexity theory is needed to individually understand any one of these systems thoroughly and how each is enriched through the new approach, the nonlinear sciences of complexity also function as a *theoretical bridge*, or linking concept between psychological, social and ecological systems, referred to by Guattari (2000) as the *three ecologies* of mind, society and nature. Nonlinear dynamical systems approaches apply to the clinical psychoanalytic encounter and to social systems just as much as to ecological networks and the Earth's climate. According to DeLanda (2005, p. 14):

> Prigogine revolutionized thermodynamics . . . by showing that the classical results were valid only for closed systems. . . . If one allows an intense flow of energy . . . [pushing] it far from equilibrium . . . instead of a unique and simple form of stability, we now have multiple coexisting forms of varying complexity (static, periodic, and chaotic attractors) . . . at a critical point called a bifurcation . . . minor fluctuations may play a crucial role. . . . Attractors and bifurcations are features of any system in which the dynamics are not only far from equilibrium but also nonlinear . . . [with] strong mutual interactions (or feedback) between components. Whether . . . composed of molecules or of living creatures, it will exhibit endogenously generated stable states, as well as sharp transitions between states, as long as there is feedback and an intense flow of energy coursing through the system.

One of the major failures of thought in relation to the climate crisis and the emergency is the fragmentation of our sciences and theories. Psychologists, psychoanalysts, sociologists, ecologists and climate scientists find it very hard to talk to one another as they lack a framework for such a conversation. Complexity science provides just such a framework. It is only with such concepts that it becomes possible to successfully *link* together our fields of understanding derived from specialist knowledge in domains such as psychology (Palombo, 2007), sociology (Stacey, 2003), biology (Sole and Goodwin, 2000), ecology (Bak, 1994; Bateson, 2000) and elsewhere. Complexity theory, along with a complex-systems based understanding of the philosophies of Deleuze and Guattari (Bonta and

Protevi, 2004; Deleuze and Guattari, 2003), help to do the 'work of linking' (Bion, 1984), connecting together disparate fields of knowledge and
approaches without each losing the specificity. This chapter will explore
these directions within ecopsychoanalysis and spell out the crucial role of
complexity theory throughout.

The ecological crisis is a failure of theory characterised by systems
blindness. Our fields of knowledge are fragmented into ever more narrowly
defined subdisciplines where specialists often have little understanding of
even closely adjacent subfields, causing serious barriers to comprehensive
research. Climate change confronts us with the disaster of this approach,
as it embodies a world of unpredictable, multiple-level, highly complex,
nonlinear interlocking systems, and to fully grasp the threat is more than
any one intellectual field can encompass. Psychoanalysis has an important
role to play in engaging with the psychology of the crisis, particularly as
concerns the affective and unconscious components, and its understanding
of defences against anxiety (Dodds, 2021, 2011; Hoggett, 2019; Weintrobe, 2012; Lertzman, 2015), yet it remains largely a psychology without ecology. There is a need for a meta-perspective able to integrate the
many disparate strands, which complexity theory can provide. However,
it is important to go beyond its application as *metaphor* towards one of
becomings, where the same dynamical processes, the same 'abstract
machine' or structure generating process, can be applied across multiple
domains.

Along with complexity theory, a complexity-based reading of Deleuze
and Guattari can also help with this work of integration. In his book *Chaosmosis*, Guattari (1995, p. 91) calls for a generalised science of ecosystems, or ecosophy, with 'resonances, alliances and feedback loops between
various regimes, signifying and non-signifying, human and non-human,
natural and cultural, material and representational'. There is as much a
need to bring nonlinear and ecological thinking into psychoanalysis as
for a psychoanalytic approach to ecology. According to Bateson (2000,
p. 468), 'the most important task today is . . . to learn to think in the new
way'. Bonta and Protevi (2004, pp. 5–7) argue that just as

> complexity theory's insistence on the natural creativity of open sys-
> tems enables Deleuze and Guattari to outflank hermeneutic humanism
> at the same time as its thematization of signs as triggers of material
> processes enables them to escape from the anti-humanist linguistic

structuralism of postmodernism, their thematizing of the subject as an emergent functional structure embedded in a series of structures enables them to escape from methodological individualism. Complexity theory . . . focuses our attention on the subject as a functional structure emerging from a multiplicity . . . historically situating . . . the signifying regime as one among several semiotic systems.

Earth as Dynamic System: Ecology at the Edge of Chaos

Climate change operates globally with effects at all scales, from psychological to planetary. We are on a collision course between an economic system predicated on unending growth on a finite planet with rapidly dwindling capacities to renew itself. This will come to an end one way or another. We are like infants unwilling to accept that the Earth-breast is not a source of infinitely increasing nourishment, unable to tolerate weaning. The global pandemic, in addition to its horror, is perhaps a chance to pause to rethink where we are heading, and to see that radical and rapid change is in fact possible and thinkable (Dodds, 2020). Complexity theory provides necessary tools to approach such a daunting task.

According to Mandelbrot (1983, p. xiii):

clouds are not spheres, mountains are not cones, coastlines are not circles, and bark is not smooth, nor does lightning travel in a straight line. . . . Nature exhibits not simply a higher degree but an altogether different level of complexity. . . . The existence of these patterns challenges us to study forms that Euclid leaves aside as being formless, to investigate the morphology of the amorphous.

Fractals exist in fractional dimensions (a coastline is more than a line but less than a surface), and are found throughout nature (e.g. trees, rivers, lungs, chromosomes, ant trails, the stock market). We can link concepts such as 'phase space' and what Deleuze and Guattari (2003) call 'abstract machines' or 'virtual diagrams', which 'lays out what an assemblage can be made out of and what it can do, not just in its current state, but in future states as it enters into becomings or transformative relations with any of the other assemblages it can reach . . . allowing for mutual interaction' (Bonta and Protevi, 2004, p. 48). Attractors include point attractors (where the system tends towards a fixed point), periodic attractors (where the system oscillates between points) and chaotic or strange attractors (where the system never settles on any specific points).

The nonlinearity of the Earth System is driven by positive feedback loops where an increase in one variable feeds back recursively, potentially producing catastrophic runaway increases if not reined in eventually by negative feedback. As Prigogine and Stengers (1984, pp. 80–81) write, the atmosphere is a self-organised system which includes strange 'objects' like the tornado, 'a sort of runaway convection current', which is "nothing more than a collection of atmospheric molecules that have organized themselves to circulate rapidly in a spiral formation'. Each of these molecules at equilibrium behaves independently, while "non-equilibrium wakes them up and introduces a coherence quite foreign to equilibrium'. A nonlinear perspective is crucial not only for climate science, but also for understanding societal collapse (Sole and Goodwin, 2000, p. 302) and the psychology of risk perception (Dodds, 2021). Linear ways of thinking imagine a simple relation between CO_2 and warming. Within certain conditions (a particular basin of attraction), this may approximate the truth. However, at a given point, a phase transition occurs and the system rapidly shifts to a new attractor. The previous 'regime' rapidly collapses to be replaced by a new system of effects. It is hard for us to grasp this – we imagine that if we keep going, warming will happen at a measured pace, and there will always be time later to turn it around. This ignores the potential of explosive positive feedbacks leading to runaway climate change, including not only meteorological and ecological loops, but also social, psychological and behavioural loops, and is therefore a fundamental failure of thought.

Positive feedbacks involved in runaway climate change (Sawaya, 2010) include, for example, *frozen ocean methane*, billions of tons of which are locked away as gas hydrate deep in the ocean only stable under specific conditions of high pressure and low temperatures, which can be released suddenly when temperatures cross a threshold; *tropical forest fires*, which become more common as temperatures increase, emitting more CO_2 and fixing less while the land also becomes hotter due to a reduction of cooling forest cover and a decreased ability to reflect heat; *melting of tundra permafrost*, which contains a third of the world's soil-bound carbon, releasing further CO_2; the *albedo effect*, where as it gets hotter more ice melts leading to more heat being absorbed rather than reflected, as ice has a higher reflection rate than earth or water; increased *methane production from bogs/peatland* as a result of warming; *decreased ocean solubility of CO$_2$* following increased temperatures, turning current regional carbon sinks into sources; and so on. Complicating the situation further are positive feedback cycles which in addition to their own effects also interact with and amplify the warming effect of other feedback loops. For example, atmospheric water vapour increases with rising temperatures (at higher temperatures the atmosphere can hold more water vapour). As well as being an important greenhouse gas itself, water vapour also amplifies the warming effects of CO$_2$ (Hansen, 2008), and those involving ice albedo and clouds.

There are also human behavioural positive feedback loops, for example, using more energy and fuel to run more air conditioning, to farm more effectively in more difficult conditions or to rebuild areas devastated by extreme weather. Other behavioural positive feedback loops are more irrational, and move into more psychoanalytic territory, such as consumerism as an addiction to deal with anxieties caused in part by overconsumption (Bodnar, 2008; Bigda-Peyton, 2004). There are negative feedback loops too, such as the spread of desertification, reflecting more heat and leading to an increased radiative cooling effect (increased temperatures result in greater heat radiating into space) and a possible mass die-off of human and animal life (reducing greenhouse gas emissions). However, both the spread of desertification and mass extinction are preferably avoided. In the end the Earth will probably survive and new life can begin again, as after previous mass extinctions (although only after millions of years of recovery time, Whiteside and Ward, 2011). Yet even this is not certain, as a runaway greenhouse effect could in the worst case leave the Earth uninhabitable, like Venus, which seems to have gone through a process such as this in the distant past, where positive feedbacks led to its oceans boiling away (Hansen, 2008).

Swarm Intelligence and Chaotic Nature

We saw in the previous chapter definitions of *self-organisation* and *emergence*. Social insects are a fascinating place to explore these concepts, and illustrate the phenomenon of *swarm intelligence*, a way of thinking about intelligence and 'mind', which may help us in our current crisis. Self-organisation involves *multistability* (the existence of several stable states the system can rapidly switch between) with structures emerging by amplification of random fluctuations, with dramatic changes at bifurcation points. Self-organisation gives rise to collective-level phenomena and structures through nonlinear dynamics and emergence, involving order out of chaos through simple interactions between units. Self-organisation is a dynamic process which can be applied equally well to multiple very different registers in physics, biology, psychology, economics, geology, sociology, history and so on. This is not a *metaphor* but rather describes one and the same dynamic process in different domains.

The concept of *stigmergy* (Grasse, 1982–1986) was developed to describe indirect communication through the environment in insect societies, where termite nest-building is coordinated not by individual workers, but by the nest itself. Each action performed by a termite modifies the stimulating configuration of the nest, triggering further actions by other termites. Stigmergy is relevant to Deleuze and Guattari's (2003, p. 68) emphasis on a signifying communication and signalling and Bateson's (2000) understanding of the environment as part of mind, with 'mind' seen as immanent to the feedback loops which don't necessarily start and finish within the surface of the body. In the case of a man cutting a tree with an axe, we can see stigmergic processes at work that Bateson (2000, p. 315) would call 'mental'.

> Each stroke of the axe is modified or corrected, according to the shape of the cut face of the tree left by the previous stroke. This self-corrective (i.e. mental) process is brought about by a total system, tree-eyes-brain-muscles-axe-stroke-tree . . . [with] the characteristics of immanent mind. . . . What is transmitted around the circuit are transforms of differences . . . a difference which makes a difference is an idea. But this is not how the average Occidental sees the sequence of tree felling. He says, 'I cut down the tree' . . . invoking the personal pronoun . . . restricting mind within the man and reifying the tree. Finally the mind itself becomes reified by the notion that, since 'self' acted upon the axe which acted upon the tree, 'self' must also be a 'thing'.

Stigmergy is a path towards complexity and can also be applied to the process of psychoanalysis. We have here not only the complex adaptive systems of the patients' mind, and the therapists', or even the co-evolving system made up by the therapeutic couple, but multiple other parts, fragments and strands get drawn into the dynamic. Each interpretation and free association can take on a life of its own within the wider self-organising network or ecology, the tick of the clock on the wall, the police siren outside, a piece of news in the morning both analyst and patient heard before the session, a small gust of wind leading the hairs on the arm to flutter and stand up. Self-organisation involves two distinct information pathways: *signals* are shaped by natural selection to convey information (e.g. ant trails from chemical pheromones), while *cues* (e.g. deer trails) are non-organic forms not acted on directly by evolution (Camazine et al., 2001, pp. 59–60). This enables non-living structures not shaped by natural selection to be incorporated into the feedback loops Bateson calls mind in a unique architecture of information flow, Deleuze and Guattari's *heterogeneous assemblages*.

Self-organisation and stigmergy illustrate the principle of *decentralised control*, pointing towards a radically different way of thinking about mind, systems and societies. Decentralised pathways include communication that is individual-individual (whether animals, cells, robots, people, etc.), group-individual (through signals and cues) or via the environment (stigmergy). There are clear cybernetic problems with central authority because it requires 'an effective communication network among individuals' and places 'formidable, if not impossible, burdens of information acquisition, processing, and transmission on the leader' (Camazine et al., 2001, p. 64). The ant colony is a *dense heterarchy* where higher levels affect lower levels and the activity thus induced in lower units feeds back to higher levels, with any member able to communicate with any other in a highly interconnected structure. DeLanda (2005, p. 93) calls such rhizomatic organisations *meshworks*, occurring at all levels of the three ecologies.

Climate change is sometimes referred to as 'climate chaos' because of the increasingly unpredictable nature of natural systems. Chaos theory shows us, paradoxically, that chaos is far from the opposite of order and structure. This position is consistent with Deleuze and Guattari (2003, p. 118) who see chaos as productive and 'defined not so much by its disorder as by the infinite speed with which every form taking shape in it vanishes . . . not a nothingness but a *virtual*, containing all possible particles and drawing out all possible forms'. Chaos is a feature of nonlinear systems, and is essential for self-organisation as the latter involves the amplification through positive feedback of random fluctuations. Why do ants regularly get 'lost'? Because through such 'errors' lost foragers sometimes find new food sources and so randomness enhances the *creativity* of a system, which Bateson (2000) calls its *ecological flexibility*. This is true in psychological, social, biological and even non-living systems (e.g. in swarm robotics, Bonabeau et al., 1999).

Living systems from brains to ant colonies attempt to balance themselves on the fractal border zone between stability and instability, the *edge of chaos*, providing maximum ecological flexibility. Dissipative systems are open systems in constant reciprocal interaction with and adaptation to their environments and exist at far-from-equilibrium conditions where they can maintain themselves within a dynamically ordered structure. The brain is a self-organising, pattern-forming system, operating close to instability points, allowing maximum flexibility to switch rapidly between states. This can be understood as a dynamic interplay between Deleuze and Guattari's (2003) territorialisation/deterritorialisation systems in constant flux. A system at the edge of chaos is described by Deleuze and Guattari as a 'rhizome' or 'consistency', in contrast to 'stratas', which are linear homeostatic systems involving negative feedback loops that damp out fluctuations and return to a stable point. Studies of EEGs, ECGs and other biorhythmic measurements show that healthy rhythms have more irregularity and complexity (turbulence), whereas unhealthy systems tend toward periodic and simplistic output (Guastello, 2004). Nonlinear processes of chaos give rise to stability by allowing the system to creatively adapt to environmental change, something increasingly urgent in our current crisis. Endogenous chaos and environmental randomness act as the 'imagination' of the system, acting as seeds from which patterns are nucleated and grow (Camazine et al., 2001, p. 26). All of this has fascinating implications for psychoanalysis.

From a clinical point of view, it is interesting to note that there can be pathological, aberrant patterns in swarms (Camazine et al., 2001, p. 282). What this research shows is that in a highly complex and interconnected system, relatively small changes of one parameter can sometimes have disastrous (and unpredictable) effects on the whole. This has important implications for the effect of climate change on the social, psychological, climate and ecological systems in Guattari's (2000) three ecologies. This can bring a complexity-based approach to Diamond's (2006) research on the collapse of civilisations, and the important roles he uncovered for systemic social interconnectivity, environmental damage and climate change. Crucially, many of these past societies entered the period of rapid collapse shortly after reaching their apogee of power and wealth, as they expanded towards the limits of what their environment and economy could sustain, evolving towards a hyper-coherent state where a failure in one part of the system led to catastrophic collapse (Sole and Goodwin, 2000, p. 302).

Mental Ecology: Nonlinear Psychoanalysis

Complexity theory provides a whole new way of thinking about psychology and psychoanalysis (Piers et al., 2007), and has been usefully applied to studying phenomena ranging from the psychoanalytic process (Boston Change Process Study Group, 2008), group analysis (Stacey, 2003), social dynamics (Dodds, 2008), schizophrenia and bipolar disorder (Hornero et al., 2006) or family system dynamics (Gottman et al., 2003). According to Guastello (2004, p. 4), 'at the broadest level of analysis . . . [it] appears to have changed the basic concept of the human mind itself'. According to Palombo (2007), complexity theory should be regarded as the parent science of psychoanalysis, replacing the limitations of nineteenth-century ideas in physics and biology embedded in psychoanalytic thought. In his book *The Emergent Ego*, he argues (Palombo, 1999, p. xviii) that the business of psychoanalysis involves 'integrating disconnected contents into the ego . . . through a process of self-organization'. Self-organisation shows how small pieces of insight assemble themselves from the bottom up into ever larger structures. Donald Meltzer (1994, p. 143) implies a similar shift in perspective for psychoanalysis when he writes that 'the problems of relationships between objects of whatever sort are more comprehensively understood in terms of communication than in terms of energy, and more accurately measured in terms of a gradient from chaos to order than in terms of closed systems of dynamic equilibria'.

Additionally, since complexity theory deals with how systems change and evolve, it is very useful for understanding the dynamics of the *psychoanalytic process*. Miller (1999, p. 364) understands psychoanalytic change as following a power law (like the grains of sand added to the sandpile), with most change confined to the local level and absorbed by the wider psychic defences. However, as the system reaches *self-organised criticality*, the tiniest local shift causes 'related schemas to destabilize and consequently loosen their ties with one another', precipitating cascades of disorganisation through the whole system leading to qualitative change.

Psychoanalysis is above all a method that allows for deep psychological change and restructuring, which, for Palombo (1999, p. 181), 'involves increasing the connectedness and complexity of the patient's mental contents'; psychoanalysis is a co-evolving system, an ecosystem stabilising near the edge of chaos.

This way of thinking can also help situate differences between conflicting psychoanalytic schools within a wider phase space of possibilities, and therefore complexity theory can become a 'selected-fact' bringing coherence to the fragmentation of psychoanalysis. According to Palombo (1999, pp. 248–249), Greenson and Zetzel 'describe a relationship between the neurotic patient and the analyst when poised near the edge of chaos', while Winnicott suggests that for some seriously ill patients 'the first stage of treatment must be the establishment of a Nash equilibrium', which in Kohut's model seems to be 'is all that is necessary for any patient'. On the other hand, obsessive patients with a dependency phobia may 'find the Nash equilibrium state itself to be threatening', so that 'the analyst's action to move the patient toward the edge of chaos is not only optimizing but essential to the continuity of the analysis'. Similarly, we can reconceptualise 'fixation' or 'regression' not as a return to an earlier state, but rather a less well-organised state of the current system where the ties that bind the elements move towards a more chaotic state, a prelude towards reorganisation (Miller, 1999). We might also consider in 'edge of chaos' terms Meltzer's (1994, p. 316) description of Klein/Bion's PS$\diamond$D as a flexible, dynamic balance on the cusp of these two attractor systems. Dreams perhaps provide the ultimate fractal graph of the psyche, a model of mind which (in health) is dynamically poised at the edge of chaos (Galatzer-Levy, 1995).

The psychoanalytic process can be viewed as moving through phase space, a co-evolving system destabilising pathological infantile attractors, which Busch (2007, p. 429) describes as 'black holes in psychological space, sucking everything in that comes near its orbit, remaining outside of awareness and thus unable to be modified by other structures'. Psychoanalysis therefore helps to develop and change rigid point and periodic attractors to more flexible and creative chaotic (strange) attractors. Defence mechanisms keep the pathological attractors simple by keeping them unconscious, closing off developmental possibilities through interactions with the outside world. As we have seen from our study of swarms, systems that inhibit information flow with their environments are unstable. This analysis can be applied to each of Guattari's three ecologies, as pathological organisations can exist on all systemic levels. This is a model of mind as an open, complex system evolving towards the edge of chaos, capable of creatively and flexibly responding to an unpredictable world, where the boundaries between self/world and self/other are seen as 'dynamically fluid and ever changing, mediated by complex, recursive feedback loops existing simultaneously at physical, social, cultural, and historical levels' (Marks-Tarlow, 2004, p. 311).

Social Ecology: Complexity and Group Dynamics

On the level of *group dynamics* (Dodds, 2008), Bion's (1961) basic assumptions can be studied as attractors towards which group life is pulled, while Foulkes's (1990) theory of group transferences as forming continuously reintegrating networks seems to call for a dynamical systems approach. This process has already begun in the field of *systems psychodynamics* (Fraha, 2004; Gould et al., 2006). Eidelson's (1997) complexity-based models suggest that by creating subsystems inside a large group, they can potentially produce pockets of collaboration that can spread, moving the larger system to a new basin of attraction. We can also compare this to Bion's (1961, pp. 125–126) description of the emotional oscillation of a basic assumption group, whose 'mad oscillations' can only be contained by bringing in 'inert' material from outside the group who do not share the emotional situation, so that the new, much larger group ceases to vibrate. However, the danger is that 'the oscillations spread to the hitherto inert', with much depending on the speed and effectiveness with which other groups are brought in, and the pre-existing emotional states of the 'outside' groups.

The nonlinear geometry of the fractal undermines a clear line between inside and outside, providing new ways to think about the individual and the group, moving from a membrane metaphor of the boundary to a multidimensional fractal borderzone. Stacey (2006, pp. 98–101) argues that Bion's (1961) work group $\Leftrightarrow$ basic assumption groups interact to create regions of stability and disintegration with potentially creative fractal regions of bounded instability at the edge of chaos between them. This move towards an ecological and complexity-based group psychoanalysis is further aided by the ecological dimension already existing in Bion's work, where he describes the way different group relations constitute commensal, symbiotic, parasitic and paranoid connections (Meltzer, 1994, p. 401). As with Bion's basic assumption theory, Jaques's (1955) social phantasy systems can be understood from a complexity perspective as emerging through the self-organisation of individual defence mechanisms, affects, fantasies and self-states, with global patterns feeding back to affect lower levels recursively, the resulting forms also interacting with wider ecological networks. This pattern embodies a system of multi-stability, with complex shifts between basins of attraction as internal objects and affects flow through the network. Thus social formations, individual mind/brains and communities can be studied as dissipative structures and swarms.

To see an example of a nonlinear social phantasy (eco)system in relation to climate change, we can consider Randall's (2005, p. 175) analysis of the 'relationship between a majority population which avoids or denies guilt and a minority into whom this same guilt can be evacuated'. The non-active majority project their environmental concern onto activists who then function as containers for the split-off collective environmental superego. By mocking those labelled as 'bearded killjoys', the external threat (climate change) and the internal threat (guilt) are both neutralised. Using a nonlinear social systems perspective allows us to see the feedback loops don't end in the first projection, but get carried around the circuit with complex social and psychological effects, reverberating back and forth in new iterations as the system moves forward in time, as other individuals and groups get drawn into existing systems, either damping down the mad oscillations (Bion) or getting swept up in nonlinear amplification effects. We should not suppose that such a gradual sharing of collective guilt would have a linear effect on the minds of activists and the public. In fact, we might rather expect to see major shifts and phase transitions between states, sometimes after long periods when the system seems stuck.

From an edge of chaos perspective, periods of instability are necessary stages on the path to greater self-organisation, with no guarantee that what will emerge will be more adaptive. We have already seen how this works on the individual psychodynamic level, and the anxieties involved during stages of disorder. Crucial for an ecopsychoanalytic conception of change is that for all of Guattari's three ecologies in certain conditions, even infinitesimally small alterations in a system's parameters can produce dramatic effects, if it has been pushed towards the state of self-organised criticality (as with Greta Thunberg, a single student who decided to sit outside parliament protesting the climate crisis rather than go to school, thereby starting a global youth movement of climate activists). The task then becomes experimental, including the search for the 'lever points' necessary to produce a major shift in the system, whether these are psychological, social or ecological, helping to overcome resistances and inertia, and opening up the possibility of more radical transformation.

> This is how it should be done: Lodge yourself on a stratum, experiment with the opportunities it offers, find an advantageous place on it, find potential movements of deterritorialization, possible lines of flight, experience them, produce flow conjunctions here and there, try out continuums of intensities segment by segment, have a small plot of new land at all times. It is through a meticulous relation with the strata that one succeeds in freeing lines of flight.
>
> (Deleuze and Guattari, 2003, p. 161)

Geophilosophy and Complexity in the Three Ecologies

In *A Thousand Plateaus*, Deleuze and Guattari (2003, p. 25) describe two kinds of science: axiomatics (royal science) and problematics (minor science). Axiomatics approaches matter through the linear stratified forms of equilibrium which can be studied through the 'molarising' process of averaging. Minor (nonlinear) science concerns 'intense' morphogenetic processes operating far from equilibrium involving lines of flight, bifurcations and becomings, opening the system's creativity through its capacity to mesh into consistencies ('networks of bodies that preserve the heterogeneity of the members even while enabling systematic emergent behavior', Bonta and Protevi, 2004, p. 192). As DeLanda (2005, p. 258) writes concerning geological processes, 'the rocks and mountains that define the most stable and durable traits of our reality . . . merely represent a local slowing down of this flowing reality . . . very slow for rocks, faster for lava'. Similarly, our own bodies and minds represent temporary 'coagulations or decelerations in the flows of biomass, genes, memes, and norms'. Languages, institutions and indeed every other aspect of our reality merely represent a 'transitory hardening' in the vast flow of becoming.

The structure-generating processes identified by complexity theory can be applied to very different domains, as we have seen. DeLanda (2005, p. 62) argues that *stratified systems* such as sedimentary rocks, species or social classes are structures created from a 'heterogeneous collection of raw materials (pebbles, genes, roles)', homogenised through sorting operations into uniform groupings, then consolidated into a more permanent state. Structures such as bureaucracies, species or sedimentary rocks therefore all share certain structural properties; as stratified systems or hierarchies, the same 'virtual diagram' applies. *Meshworks*, on the other hand, are formed differently. Igneous rocks, for example, are formed by intense heterogeneous flows of magma formed from multiple components with different crystallisation thresholds. As it cools, different elements separate through sequential crystallisation, with elements solidifying earlier serving as containers for those that crystallise later, resulting in complex, heterogeneous interlocking crystals, giving granite its superior strength (DeLanda, 2005, p. 64). Further complexities arise through 'intercalary elements' (comparable to the stigmergetic processes discussed earlier) involving, for example, reactions between liquid magma and already crystallised components, nucleation events and 'defects' inside crystals which promote growth from within, and can generate self-organised pattern formations such as spirals.

The processes underlying meshworks and strata formation can be found in all registers. The distinction between these two processes is, like the length of the fractal coastline, dependent on scale. For example, even animals in total reproductive isolation may exchange genetic materials via inheritable viruses. The evolutionary process is therefore more of a meshwork or rhizome than a strictly branching tree, with viruses allowing the exchange of genetic material between distant taxonomic groups, viruses themselves existing on the uncanny borderzone between life and nonlife (Dodds, 2020). The meshwork/hierarchy distinction is therefore better viewed as the 'molarising' and 'molecularising' potentials of any given system. As DeLanda (2005, p. 260) writes, 'meshworks give rise to hierarchies and hierarchies to meshworks . . . undergoing processes of destratification as well as restratification, as its proportions of homogeneous and heterogeneous components change'.

Deleuze and Guattari, and also Bateson, point us towards a new ecological way of thinking about mind. Bateson (2000) provides a way to understand how fallacies in the ecology of ideas can have direct and catastrophic results on the social and ecological registers. As Bateson (2000, p. 492) writes: 'There is an ecology of bad ideas, just as there is an ecology of weeds, and it is characteristic of the system that basic error propagates itself. It branches out like a rooted parasite through the tissues of life'. For Bateson (2000, p. 274), 'mental characteristics of the system are immanent, not in some part, but in the system as a whole'. The mind he describes is not transcendent but immanent in a network of causal pathways. Following psychoanalysis, these include unconscious as well as conscious networks, and those internal and external to the physical organism. Similarly, for Deleuze and Guattari the self is precariously balanced between forces both above (the 'collective assemblages of enunciation' which constrain but also enable it) and below (the 'larval subjects' out of which it forms through emergent processes of self-organisation). Thus, the schizoanalytic unconscious is 'an acentered system . . . a machinic network of finite automata', a self-organising swarm (Deleuze and Guattari, 2003, p. 18).

An acrobat on a high wire, in order not to fall, requires maximum freedom to move from one position of instability to another (Bateson, 2000, p. 506). Like the patient stuck on a local optima unable or unwilling to cross the threshold to a more adaptive peak, civilisations and species have found themselves in dangerous dead ends, unable to change. Ecopsychoanalysis, drawing on the tools and ideas of nonlinear science, understands that our world is governed by nonlinear dynamics, so that the prediction and control promised by Enlightenment rationality will always remain, to some degree, illusory. Instead, we need to engage with the creativity of the Earth and explore the potential for self-organisation and ecological thinking on all scales. Perhaps it is in the very severity of our desperate situation in the face of a chaotic Earth that a great opportunity lies for re-imagining the human and our place in the world.

References

Bak, P. (1994). Self-organized criticality: A holistic view of nature. In Cowan, G., Pines, D. & Meltzer, D. (eds.), *Santa Fe Institute Studies in the Sciences of Complexity, Proceedings Volume XIX. Complexity: Metaphors, Models, and Reality* (pp. 477–496). Redwood City, CA: Addison Wesley.

Bateson, G. (2000). *Steps Towards an Ecology of Mind*. Chicago and London: University of Chicago Press.

Bigda-Peyton, F. (2004). When drives are dangerous: Drive theory and resource over-consumption. *Modern Psychoanalysis*, 29, 251–270.

Bion, W. (1961). *Experiences in Groups and Other Papers*. London and New York: Routledge.

———. (1984). *Second Thoughts: Selected Papers on Psychoanalysis*. London: Karnac.

Bodnar, S. (2008). Wasted and bombed: Clinical enactments of a changing relationship to the Earth. *Psychoanalytic Dialogues*, 18, 484–512.

Bonabeau, E., Dorigo, M. & Theraulaz, G. (1999). *Swarm Intelligence: From Natural to Artificial Systems*. New York: Oxford University Press.

Bonta, M. & Protevi, J. (2004). *Deleuze and Geophilosophy: A Guide and Glossary*. Edinburgh: Edinburgh University Press.

Boston Change Process Study Group & Nahum, J. (2008). Forms of relational meaning: Issues in the relations between the implicit and reflective-verbal domains. *Psychoanalytic Dialogues*, 18(2), 125±148.

Busch, F. (2007). 'I Noticed': The emergence of self-observation in relationship to pathological attractor sites. *International Journal of Psycho-Analysis*, 88, 423±441.

Camazine, S., Deneubourg, J.-L., Franks, N., Sneyd, J., Theraulaz, G. & Bonabeau, E. (2001). *Self Organization in Biological Systems*. Princeton and Oxford: Princeton University Press.

DeLanda, M. (2005). *A Thousand Years of Nonlinear History*. New York: Swerve.

Deleuze, G. & Guattari, F. (2003). *A Thousand Plateaus: Capitalism and Schizophrenia*. Minneapolis and London: University of Minnesota Press.

Diamond, J. (2006). *Collapse: How Societies Choose to Fail or Survive*. London: Penguin.

Dodds, J. (2008). Artificial group psychodynamics: Emergence of the collective. In Dietrich, F. & Zucker, B. (eds.), *Simulating the Mind: A Technical Neuropsychoanalytical Approach*. Vienna and New York: Springer.

———. (2011). *Psychoanalysis and Ecology at the Edge of Chaos: Complexity Theory, Deleuze|Guattari and Psychoanalysis for a Climate in Crisis*. Sussex and New York: Routledge.

———. (2012). The ecology of phantasy: Ecopsychoanalysis and the three ecologies. In Rust, M. & Totten, N. (ed.), *Vital Signs: Psychological Responses to Ecological Crisis*. London: Karnac.

———. (2013). Minding the ecological body: Neuropsychoanalysis and ecopsychoanalysis. *Frontiers in Psychology*, 2013.

———. (2019). *Otto Fenichel and Ecopsychoanalysis in the Anthropocene*. Psychoanalytic Perspectives.

———. (2020). Elemental catastrophe: Ecopsychoanalysis and the viral uncanny of COVID-19. *Stillpoint: Digital Magazine in the Eye of the Storm*, 2020.

———. (2021). The psychology of climate anxiety. *BJPsych Bull*, 45(4), 222–226.

Dodds, J. & Poenaru, L. (2021). The future of psychoanalysis at the edge of chaos. In *Analysis,* 2021. Retrieved from https://www.academia.edu/46882874/

The_future_of_psychoanalysis_at_the_edge_of_chaos_Interview_Joseph_ Dodds_Liviu_Poenaru

Eidelson, R. (1997). Complex adaptive systems in the behavioral and social sciences. *Review of General Psychology*, 1(1), 42–71.

Foulkes, S. (1990). *Selected Papers of S.H. Foulkes: Psychoanalysis and Group Analysis*. London: Karnac.

Fraha, A. (2004). Systems psychodynamics: The formative years of an interdisciplinary field at the Tavistock Institute. *History of Psychology*, 7(1), 65–84.

Galatzer-Levy, R. (1995). Psychoanalysis and dynamical systems theory: Prediction and self similarity. *Journal of the American Psychoanalytic Association*, 43, 1085–1113.

Gottman, J., Murray, J., Swanson, C., Tyson, R. & Swanson, K. (2003). *The Mathematics of Marriage: Dynamic Nonlinear Models*. Cambridge, Massachusetts: MIT Press.

Gould, L., Stapley, R. & Stein, M. (Eds.). (2006). *The Systems Psychodynamics of Organizations: Integrating Group Relations, Psychoanalytic, and Open Systems Perspectives*. London: Karnac.

Grasse, P.-P. (1982–1986). *Termitologia. Vol. 1: Anatomie Physiologie Reproduction; Vol 2: Foundation des Sociétés Construction; Vol. 3: Comportement Socialité Écologie Évolution Systématique*. Paris and New York: Masson.

Guastello, S. (2004). Progress in applied nonlinear dynamics. *Nonlinear Dynamics, Psychology and Life Sciences*, 8(1), 1–15.

Guattari, F. (1995). *Chaosmosis: An Ethico-aesthetic Paradigm*. Bloomington: Indiana University Press.

———. (2000). *The Three Ecologies*. London: Athlone.

Hansen, J. (2008). *Climate Threat to the Planet: Implications for Energy Policy and Intergenerational Justice*. Bjerknes Lecture, American Geophysical Union.

Hoggett, P. (2019). *Climate Psychology: On Indifference to Disaster*. London: Palgrave.

Hornero, R., Jimeno, N., Sanchez, C., Poza, J. & Aboy, M. (2006). Variability, regularity, and complexity of time series generated by schizophrenic patients and control subjects. *IEEE Transactions on Biomedical Engineering*, 53(2), 216–218.

Jaques, E. (1955). Social systems as a defence against persecutory and depressive anxiety. In Klein, M., Heimann, P. & Money-Kyrle, R. (eds.), *New Directions in Psychoanalysis* (pp. 478–498). London: Karnac.

Lertzman, R. (2015). *Environmental Melancholia: Psychoanalytic Dimensions of Engagement*. London and New York: Routledge.

Mandelbrot, B. (1983). *The Fractal Geometry of Nature*. San Francisco: W. H. Freeman.

Marks-Tarlow, T. (2004). The self as a dynamical system. *Nonlinear Dynamics, Psychology, and Life Sciences*, 3(4), 311–345.

Meltzer, D. (1994). *Sincerity and Other Works: Collected Papers of Donald Meltzer*. London: Karnac.

Miller, M. (1999). Chaos, complexity, psychoanalysis. *Psychoanalytic Psychology*, 16(3), 355–379.

Palombo, S. (1999). *The Emergent Ego: Complexity and Coevolution in the Psychoanalytic Process*. Madison: International Universities Press.

———. (2007). Complexity theory as the parent science of psychoanalysis. In Piers, C., Muller, P. & Brent, J. (eds.), *Self-Organizing Complexity in Psychological Systems*. Plymouth: Jason Aronson.

Piers, C., Muller, P. & Brent, J. (Eds.). (2007). *Self-Organizing Complexity in Psychological Systems*. Plymouth: Jason Aronson.

Prigogine, I. & Stengers, I. (1984). *Order Out Of Chaos: Man's New Dialogue With Nature*. New York: Bantam Books.

Randall, R. (2005). A new climate for psychotherapy? *Psychotherapy and Politics International*, 3(3), 165–179.

Sawaya, R. (2010). The runaway effects that could accelerate global warming.

Sole, R. & Goodwin, B. (2000). *Signs of Life: How Complexity Pervades Biology*. New York: Basic Books.

Stacey, R. (2003). *Complexity and Group Processes: A Radically Social Understanding of Individuals*. New York: Brunner-Routledge.

———. (2006). Complexity at the edge of the basic-assumption group. In Gould, L., Stapley, R. & Stein, M. (eds.), *The Systems Psychodynamics of Organizations: Integrating Group Relations, Psychoanalytic, and Open Systems Perspectives* (pp. 91–114). London: Karnac.

Weintrobe, S. (Ed.). (2012). *Engaging with Climate Change Psychoanalytic and Interdisciplinary Perspectives*. Hove and New York: Routledge.

Whiteside, J. & Ward, P. (2011). Ammonoid diversity and disparity track episodes of chaotic carbon cycling during the early Mesozoic. *Geology*, 39(2), 99–102.

Part 3

Epigenetics

Chapter 5

Psychoanalysis and Epigenetics

Roberto Colangeli, PhD

Introduction

This chapter aims to introduce the epigenetics model, to address the most up-to-date research in the field of epigenetics, and to relate this research to the mental health profession of psychoanalysis. In the paragraphs that follow I will show how epigenetics validates the psychoanalytic concept that most human psychological conditions, such as psychological trauma, result from environmental factors that affect physiology and genetics, not the other way around. I will also discuss the role that intergenerational transmission of trauma plays in psychoanalysis and demonstrate, using experimental models in animals and studies in humans, how psychological trauma can trigger changes in the DNA that can be transmitted to the next generation.

Recent publications have helped define the link between the mother's adverse psychological condition and the genetic, physiological changes of the fetus. These changes can be followed even after birth and be associated with psychological outcomes such as depression and anxiety.

To conclude, I will discuss the possibility that psychological therapies can alter and reverse epigenetic trauma. Recent data suggest the possibility that psychotherapies can revert epigenetic modifications caused by traumatic events and that they can also regulate stress hormones and different neurotransmitters that modulate many aspects of human behavior.

History and Evolution of Genetics

In the middle of the last century, Gregor Mendel conducted a series of experiments on the pea plant, and the results of these experiments established many of the genetic rules of heredity; this is now referred to as Mendelian

DOI: 10.4324/9781003271499-9

inheritance. Mendel's work was recognized in 1900 when his experiments were rediscovered by Wilhelm Johannsen; Johannsen renamed the findings in 1909 with the term "genes." In 1911, Johannsen introduced the difference between genotype (the particular set of genes contained in the DNA of an organism) and phenotype (the set of observable characteristics of an organism, such as its morphology, physiology, and behavior). The combination of Mendelian genetics and the Darwinian theory of evolution led to the synthetic theory of evolution during the 1930s and 1940s (Keller, 2000).

Significant developments continued to occur from mid-century onward. The discovery in 1953 of the double-helix molecular structure of DNA (deoxyribonucleic acid) profoundly changed genetics, and a new central dogma of molecular biology postulated that hereditary "biological information" flows in a single direction: from DNA transcribed to RNA (ribonucleic acid), which is in turn translated into proteins. With all of these developments, it is little wonder that James Watson said, "we used to think our fate was in our stars. Now we know that, in large measure, our fate is in our genes" (Jaroff, 1989, p. 67). Watson was referring to a view of humans that is strictly dependent on the nature and functions of our genes.

In 1990, the Human Genome Project was launched with the aim to sequence and locate all human genes. As Watson declared, the hope was to decipher "the language of life" and the key to many diseases. The project ended in 2003, and only 20,000 genes encoding proteins were found; to offer some perspective on the findings, an earthworm has more than 19,000 genes (Collins, 2010). There were too few genes to explain the complexity of human physiology, and Francis Collins, the acting director of the Human Genome Project, acknowledged a decade after sequencing the human genome, the promises of this project remain unfulfilled. Another surprising finding was that only 1.5 percent of the DNA is directly related to protein synthesis (coding DNA). Earlier, the remaining DNA was mostly considered "junk DNA" or noncoding DNA because its function was largely unknown (Collins, 2010). More recently, however, this "junk DNA" has been found to play a crucial role in human genetics. This noncoding DNA regulates the function of the coding DNA itself. This discovery radically changed the concept of gene coding proteins as fundamental units of the genome that are responsible for hereditary biological traits.

It appeared clear that the single gene was not alone responsible for human biology's complexity, but the regulation of each of the human genes offered an illuminated source of genetic diversity. This can explain why humans are different from each other even if their DNA sequence is 99.6 percent identical (Collins, 2010), or why monozygotic twins who supposedly share identical genes can have very different morphological and psychological traits.

For years, biologists have accepted that DNA and genes were responsible for people having particular body shapes, personalities, and diseases. Scientists argued that genes alone could determine intelligence or the mutations responsible for poverty, violence, and crime. This limited view of human behavior was opposed by psychoanalysts, who proposed that our minds continually evolve and change in response to our interaction with the environment and others. Psychoanalysis has been particularly critical about the biological concept of gene irreversibility (specific and irreversible DNA mutations), especially if this concept is used to justify human behavior. Psychoanalysts had argued that if the gene irreversibility theory is correct, then the only option is to be resigned to human behavioral problems and limitations with no hope to change or modify them.

The last few decades have seen an increasing understanding that gene regulation in humans and the environment are deeply linked. Many studies have shown that changes in the environment can turn genes on or off and finely regulate their expression. These interactions between the environment and genes are often transitory and reversible, depending on the need to respond to different environmental conditions. This new branch of biology is now called epigenetics.

What Is Epigenetics?

Epigenetics, from the Greek *epi* (επί – over, above) refers to changes in gene expression without any change to the primary DNA sequence (Wolffe and Matzke, 1999). In general terms, epigenetics is defined as the alterations in the gene expression profile that are not caused by changes in the DNA sequence (Peschansky and Wahlestedt, 2014). Epigenetic processes, far from being rare, are ubiquitous in the development of organisms. For example, the process of cell differentiation that involves the transformation of a single cell or totipotent zygote (with the ability to be any cell type) into each of the more than 200 different specialized cells in the human body is mostly epigenetic. In addition, epigenetic modification of gene expression is universal across all living kingdoms. It has been observed in plants (Cubas et al., 1999), yeasts (Halfmann et al., 2012), protozoans (Jordan et al., 2013), and humans.

Epigenetic mechanisms explain how it is possible that the environment can modify neural and behavioral functions. Genes can be turned "on" and "off" via various epigenetic mechanisms, such as DNA methylation (chemical groups are added to the DNA molecule), histone modifications (the structure that can change gene expression), and small RNA (small RNA that can inhibit the expression of target genes), resulting in phenotypic changes (Goldberg et al., 2007). The effects of these mechanisms and the regulatory enzymes involved in biochemical pathways are key epigenetic processes (Ptashne, 2007). Further, one of the most remarkable epigenetics features is that its effects can be inherited by the next generation, unlike other gene regulation mechanisms (Heard and Martienssen, 2014).

In summary, epigenetics involves studying how the environment shapes our genes (Francis, 2011). Our modern understanding of epigenetics continues to expand on all the initial discoveries, as interest in epigenetics has exploded in recent years.

Trauma and Epigenetics

Trauma is one of the cornerstones of psychoanalytic theory. The French neurologist Jean-Martin Charcot and later, Freud, point to trauma as the origin of all mental illness (Freud, 1982). In 1892 Freud stated, "A trauma would have to be defined as an *accretion of excitation* in the nervous system, *which the latter has been unable to dispose of adequately by motor reaction*" (Freud, 1892, p. 137, emphasis original). Freud utilizes the concept of trauma in several of his works, such as in his original formulations of hysteria (Breuer & Freud, 1893-1895), in *Beyond the Pleasure Principle* (Freud, 1920), in *The Ego and the Id* (Freud, 1923), and in later writings. In Freud's view, trauma was generated by a particularly overwhelming stimulus such as physical, mental, or emotional abuse.

An exception in this period is the work on childhood trauma and its impact on personality and analytic treatment by Sándor Ferenczi. Ferenczi suggested that disregarding external realities in favor of the neurotic's phenomena from inner dispositions may lead to wrong conclusions about a patient (Ferenczi, 1955). His claims directly contrast with Freud's idea that memories of sexual abuse are based on instinct-driven fantasies. Because of this dispute and Ferenczi's unconventional methods, Ferenczi's thoughts were rejected and disregarded within the psychoanalytic community for a long time.

After Freud, the psychoanalytic theoretical discussion about trauma became marginal. Even if several trauma concepts were formulated – projective identification by Melanie Klein (Klein, 1946); containing alpha and beta elements by Bion (Bion, 1962); Bowlby's attachment theory (Bowlby, 1958); new approaches to language by Jacques Lacan (Lacan, 1968) – these theories did not fundamentally change the original Freud formulation of trauma.

Significative changes in the theory of trauma's framework had to wait until the 1940s and 1950s. The psychoanalytic, interpersonal approach of Harry Sullivan shifted the experience from "inside" the patient to the interactions with other people. Sullivan's view was that because individuals can't be separated from their environment, human personalities are formed in interpersonal interactions with others. Consequently, the understanding of trauma shifted to the interaction between people rather than the internal Freudian drives.

During the 1950s, studies on the early development of the child and the relationship with the mother brought new insights into the conception of trauma (Khan, 1963). Notably, Balint (1969) was among the first to revisit Ferenczi's theories on trauma (Ferenczi, 1988). Balint postulated that the traumatic effect of a situation depends on whether a relationship existed between the child and the traumatic object. All of the more modern theories of trauma strongly emphasize the role and the influence of the external world, focusing in particular on childhood trauma and issues of attachment and separation more than on the development of internal factors (Siebold, 2013; Massie and Szajnberg, 2006).

This new environmental conception of trauma is no longer seen as a monolithic entity but as events or processes that vary with the age, developmental level, and mental capacity of those affected. Today trauma is understood, at the individual level, as a subjective event. This new way of thinking about trauma complicates the way we speak about or categorize it. Despite this, psychoanalytic literature has developed a series of terms to specify and distinguish between different trauma types. Thus, we can refer to childhood or adult trauma (Boschan, 2008), shock trauma (Chaudoye et al., 2017), massive psychic trauma (Mucci, 2014), cumulative trauma (Khan, 1963), dissociative trauma (van der Kolk, 2000), and so forth.

A recent development in science has also helped to better understand trauma on the human brain and DNA. Several studies have shown the effects of environmental stress on the brain at the molecular and cellular level (Jackowski et al., 2009). Studies in infants have demonstrated the strong correlation between trauma in the developing brain of the infant and damages in the limbic system, which was associated with future aggressive behavior and affective dysregulation (Schore, 2009). Additionally, chemical changes in the brain due to prolonged traumatic stress have been shown to induce DNA structure changes and mutations.

Although it is challenging to directly correlate these types of psychological trauma with modifications sustained by DNA, many pieces of evidence have suggested that a correlation does indeed exist (De Bellis and Zisk, 2014). For example, cumulative trauma, a term introduced by Khan (1963) that refers to small but recurrent inner stresses, is mirrored by the small but continuous external stresses induced by the environment (such as pollution, chemicals, smoke, alcohol, etc.) on DNA.

The discovery of epigenetic mechanisms made it clear that environmental and psychological factors can directly affect DNA. Changes in the DNA molecule were found to be transitory and dependent on environmental circumstances. In this new scenario, rather than scientists claiming that psychoanalysis is irrelevant, scientific findings support its role as much more significant. It has even been suggested that psychotherapy could be regarded as an "epigenetic drug" (Stahl, 2012).

This emphasis on behavior makes it more evident than ever that psychoanalysis can positively reduce the expression of DNA damaged by trauma (Kader et al., 2018; Provenzi et al., 2019). In the following paragraphs, I will describe a few key experiments in detail, chosen from many, which elucidate the relationship between epigenetics, trauma in animal models, humans, and the transmission of behaviors to subsequent generations.

Animal Models

Animal models have been used to study the correlation between environmental stress (trauma) and modifications of the DNA structure. One of the most well-known experiments has been described by Francis et al. (1999) and later expanded by Weaver et al. (2004) using a rat model.

In these experiments, differences in behavior, hypothalamic-pituitary-adrenal (HPA), and DNA methylation were observed between rat pups that have been exposed to mothers with high licking/grooming and arched-back nursing (LG-ABN) compared to mothers with a low LG-ABN behavior. As adults, rat pups exposed to high LG-ABN mothers demonstrated the ability to tolerate mild stressors and show less intense HPA responses to stress than the rat pups exposed to low LG-ABN mothers. These results suggested that the differences between rat pups exposed to high and low LG-ABN were due to maternal behavior.

DNA methylation was measured in both groups of rats. Results showed that in rats exposed to high LG-ABN, DNA demethylation increased the glucocorticoid receptor (GR) in the hippocampus; GR is a protein present in almost every cell in the body that binds explicitly to the hormone cortisol and is critical for the somatic stress response, among other functions. Weaver et al. (2004) were also interested in addressing if the behavioral mode of transmission (DNA demethylation) was reversible or not.

To address this, cross-fostering with the offspring of high and low LG-ABN mothers was performed. In this experiment, the female biological offspring of low LG-ABN raised by high LG-ABN mothers showed significantly less fear than low LG-ABN offspring raised by low LG-ABN mothers. The opposite result was obtained using high LG-ABN females raised by low LG-ABN mothers, and control groups were used as positive and negative controls (Weaver et al., 2004). These set of experiments have been recapitulated by numerous other investigations (Liu et al., 1997; Caldji et al., 1998; Dunn and Berridge, 1990; Hutchinson et al., 2012).

A more recent set of studies aimed to address if the DNA methylation observed after trauma could be found in the germline and thus be transmitted to offspring. In the classic experiment conducted by Mansuy et al. (cited in Gapp et al., 2016), trauma was induced by maternal separation in mice (MSUS), and a light-dark box was used to measure murine ability to tolerate stress. Stressed mice (generation 1) could stay longer in the light (because they were more stressed) than non-stressed mice, demonstrating that stressful conditions could affect behavioral changes.

To address if trauma from MSUS could be transmitted from generation 1 to generation 2 of mice, generation 2 mice were raised with and without mothers who were exposed to a foot-shock, which could be terminated by a nose-poke into a hole. Generation 2 MSUS (traumatized) mice had a shorter time to nose-poke (receiving fewer foot-shocks) than fostered generation 2 mice (non-traumatized), suggesting a more active coping response.

To link the behavioral effect of trauma to DNA changes, methylation in sperm from MSUS generation 1 males was analyzed and compared with controls. Results showed that DNA methylation was significantly decreased in MSUS generation 1 compared to the controls. A similar effect was also observed in the generation 2 offspring of MSUS males (Gapp et al., 2016). Overall, numerous animal studies provide evidence that epigenetic modification can be transmitted through generations via gametes (egg or sperm) (Bock et al., 2016; Harker et al., 2015; Finegood et al., 2017).

Epigenetics in Humans

Studies of human epigenetics are still at an early stage. While more is known about the role of epigenetics in human diseases such as cancer or autoimmune diseases, less is known about the correlation between psychological disorders and trauma; however, in the last few years, several studies have indicated a correlation between epigenetics and trauma in humans. For ethical reasons, research in humans' behavioral epigenetics is more challenging than in animals because of the inaccessibility of living tissues such as the brain. Alternative approaches include studies that use human postmortem brain samples or neurons produced from somatic tissues. The main problem with these methodologies is the lack of an individual's experiences. Recently, evidence has suggested a direct correlation between epigenetic changes in the brain and change in specific markers in blood and saliva that can be more easily measured.

In a healthy individual, trauma or stress conditions primarily affect the hypothalamic-pituitary-adrenal (HPA) axis. This activation results in the secretion of a cascade of hormones, which ends up causing the adrenal gland to release cortisol into the bloodstream. Cortisol is a well-known hormone involved in a fight or flight response to manage the stressor. The cortisol binds specific DNA fragments called glucocorticoid receptors (GRs) concentrated in the hippocampus. This binding inhibits the HPA axis and subsequently diminishes the body's response to stress conditions (Jacobson and Sapolsky, 1991). Several studies have suggested that the number of GRs is reduced in subjects with a traumatic history (Perroud et al., 2014; Conradt et al., 2013). The reduced number of GRs translates into dysregulation of the HPA axis and an increase of cortisol levels in response to stressors, making it more challenging to manage and cope with trauma (Ohlstein et al., 1989).

Another target that has been recently used as a marker of trauma in humans is that of small RNAs. This class of RNAs is defined as short, non-coding RNA molecules that can inhibit the expression of target genes. Small RNAs can influence the amygdala, hippocampus, and prefrontal cortex, which are interrelated in posttraumatic stress syndrome and posttraumatic stress disorder pathophysiology (Shin et al., 2006; Herringa et al., 2013). Hormones, such as cortisol, small RNAs, DNA methylation (DNAm), and the number of GRs can be measured indirectly, using blood or saliva.

Many studies on epigenetics and trauma have targeted specific groups with a clear trauma history, such as Holocaust survivors and those living with PTSD (Walton et al., 2016; Braun et al., 2019). Posttraumatic stress disorder (PTSD) is an acquired psychiatric disorder with functionally impairing physiological and psychological symptoms following traumatic exposure. Diagnosis of PTSD is based on criteria such as flashbacks, nightmares, avoidance behaviors, negative mood/thoughts, and alterations in arousal. Suicide rates are elevated in PTSD patients in most studies, although the statistical relationships are complicated, especially since comorbid psychiatric diagnoses are frequently present. Epigenetic studies have identified epigenetic changes in DNA methylation (DNAm) associated with PTSD. Previous studies using candidate gene and genome-wide approaches have identified epigenetic changes in DNAm related to PTSD.

In a recent study, Logue et al. (2020) hypothesized that differences in DNAm levels in genes associated with the hypothalamic-pituitary-adrenal (HPA) axis could be detected in subjects with PTSD. In this study, blood samples were used to extract and purify DNA from individuals with PTSD (a cohort of veterans) and controls. The entire human DNA was sequenced and showed a significant difference between DNAm in PTSD subjects than in controls. Other studies have demonstrated that DNAm also correlates with the social environment (Turecki and Meaney, 2016). For example, McGowan et al (2009) and Lam et al (2012) found that child maltreatment was associated with increased DNAm within the hippocampal tissue of adults who committed suicide. Lam et al. (2012) have shown that early life traumatic events were correlated with DNAm in peripheral blood samples. More recently, Dunn et al. (2019) found that most DNAm in the blood samples from a maltreated child cohort from the UK were associated with adversity occurring at ≤3 years of age compared with more recent events.

These studies suggest that the timing of certain early experiences plays a role in biological embedding, although we note that the biological embedding of experience can occur across the lifespan (Sanz et al., 2020). These studies that rely on using blood samples, rather than needing to analyze living brains, demonstrate a correlation between epigenetic changes in trauma patients.

Intergenerational Transmission of Trauma and Epigenetics in Humans

In the last few decades, compelling scientific evidence has corroborated the link between environmental factors (such as climate, nutrition, and experiences) and epigenetic changes in the DNA. Several studies have recently focused on the possibility that such DNA modifications can be transmitted to the next generation, validating the psychoanalytic concept of the intergenerational transmission of trauma.

Intergenerational transmission of trauma refers to the process where traumatic experiences are passed on by a patient to their children. The possibility of transmission of trauma from one generation to another was recognized early by Ferenczi (1955). Ferenczi, in his dialogue of the unconscious intersubjective, realized the importance of social trauma in the individual's life and the possibility that such trauma could be passed to the following generation.

Since Ferenczi, a growing number of studies have focused on intergenerational trauma in children with parents who have a history of trauma (Fonagy, 1999; Iyengar et al., 2014). The literature concludes that aspects of the effects of massive trauma experienced by survivor groups have been observed to occur in their children and subsequent generations.

While several studies in animal models have demonstrated the effects of trauma on DNA and the ability of these DNA modifications to be reversible and transmissible to the next generation, less is known about trauma and epigenetics in humans. Studies involving personal trauma history or a disaster like the Dutch Hunger Winter, the Holocaust, and the Quebec ice storm offer the possibility of studying the epigenetic mechanisms associated with the biological embedding of experience.

In one study, Feig's laboratory (Dickson et al., 2018) studied a group of men with different levels of early life trauma (assessed using psychological questionnaires) for alterations of small RNA in the sperm. The expression of two small RNAs present in the sperm was much lower among men with the most extensive trauma than men with the least trauma (Dickson et al., 2018). This result has been supported by findings in the sperm of animal models, where exposure to early life stress leads offspring of mice to experience increased anxiety for at least three generations (Wu et al., 2014). Several other studies have shown similar results (Bohacek et al., 2018; Sharma et al., 2016; Chan et al., 2018). McGowan et al. (2009) examined GR levels in hippocampal samples obtained from suicide victims who had a history of childhood abuse as well as control subjects who were negative for a history of childhood abuse and who had died suddenly of unrelated causes. Results indicated that GR expression was decreased in samples from suicide victims with a history of childhood abuse compared with controls.

In better understanding the transmission of trauma, it is important to have reliable studies that compare more than one generation (Yehuda et al., 2014). In a recent study, Yehuda et al. (2016) focused on the methylation of a protein regulating GP (known to regulate the HPA axis) in Holocaust survivors and their offspring. This study found Holocaust survivors and their offspring to have the same DNA methylation changes. This epigenetic change was not present in a control group of individuals with no history of trauma. Therefore, this demonstrates a direct association between trauma, epigenetic changes, and transmission of trauma through DNA modifications in humans (Yehuda et al., 2016).

A similar study explored cortisol production and methylation of the FKBP5 gene in blood samples from Holocaust survivors and in their adult offspring. This study found similar reduction methylation in the FKBP5 gene and cortisol level in both groups compared to controls (Yehuda et al., 2016).

Another study has focused on the Dutch Hunger Winter, a period of famine at the end of World War II that gave rise to a range of adverse metabolic and mental health outcomes for people later in life. In this study, blood samples from children born to women exposed to the Dutch Hunger Winter showed reduced methylation within a gene implicated in growth and metabolism.

In addition, the possibility that psychological trauma or stress can be transmitted to offspring in humans is not only limited to change in DNA in the germinal cells; it can also directly affect the human fetus. A study has shown that children of women who were pregnant during the Quebec ice storm and who exhibited a high level of stress (two questionnaires were used to assess stress levels) have much higher DNA methylation than children conceived in the same period from mothers who were not exposed to stressful conditions during the pregnancy (Cao-Lei et al., 2014).

Some of these studies present limitations; for example, some of the biological samples may not be available from before the onset of the traumatic event, which complicates the analysis to determine if the DNA changes occurred in response to the experience. Even for studies with samples collected before and after the traumatic event, a control group is needed to distinguish the effects of the exposure from biological processes that could already be in motion, unrelated to the exposure of interest. Thus, it is challenging to separate the influence of a single traumatic event and correlate this with epigenetic changes. Nevertheless, these studies strongly suggest a possibility that trauma not only affects DNA regulation but that these changes can be passed from one generation to another. Going forward, more studies will need to be designed that gather sample sizes of larger, more comprehensive cohorts and that utilize advances in technology, such as the rapid and inexpensive methods to sequence the human genome.

Epigenetic Effects of the Psychological Environment on the Fetus and Early Years of Infancy

The relatively new science of epigenetics has stimulated interest and conversation among different fields of science. Epigenetics has interjected in a long-lasting conversation about the overlap and interplay of nature versus nurture; this interjection is especially highlighted in the dialogue between epigenetics and the early development of trauma in the fetus and in the early years of infancy. During fetal and infant development, the brain is rapidly changing, leading to proliferation and refinement of neural pathways. The sensitive period created by this time of neuronal plasticity establishes a window of opportunity during which experiences can exert long-term effects.

The relation between the mother's physical and mental health and the fetus is well known (John, 2019). Prenatal stress has been widely associated with several short- and long-term pathological factors, such as diabetes and cardiovascular disease (Kaur et al., 2013). The experience of severe stressors during gestation, such as exposure to a natural disaster or terrorist attack, has been associated with preterm birth, reduced birth weight, and a smaller head circumference (Fernandez Arias et al., 2019).

Epigenetics and the Fetus

In 1981, David Barker presented clear evidence of a correlation between low birth weight and adult onset diseases such as stroke, hypertension, coronary heart disease, and type 2 diabetes (Barker et al., 1989). The "Barker hypothesis" (today better known as prenatal programming or fetal programming) refers to the environment's influence on the fetus's development. Barker postulated that the development of organs and functions undergo programming during embryonic and fetal life, influencing physiological and metabolic responses into adulthood. Recently, Barker expanded his original hypothesis to include different alterations of the fetal environment such as nutrition, endocrine status, toxic chemicals, and psychological trauma that can cause changes in the fetal environment and predispose individuals to later onset diseases and brain adaptation to different stresses and traumas (Nicoletto and Rinaldi, 2011).

The fetal programming hypothesis has been studied intensely in animals (McArdle et al., 2006) and applied to human populations (Egliston et al., 2007). The more recent advances in epigenetics have allowed scientists to address and establish correlations between the mother's psychological state and the fetus's effects at the DNA level.

Two dominant fetal programming models are the cumulative stress model (a disease-focused approach) and the match-matching model (an evolutionary-developmental approach). The cumulative stress model assumption is that developmental exposures to stress can be cumulative, which leads to disruptions of brain structure and function, resulting in dysregulation of physiological mediators. A fundamental premise of cumulative stress models is that accidents and other environmental insults limit, rather than adaptively calibrate, individual development (Shonkoff et al., 2012).

The match-matching model uses evolutionary models to explain how a developing fetus adapts to different stresses in anticipation of the postnatal environment (Nederhof and Schmidt, 2012). Signals, such as high levels of stress hormone, from the extrauterine environment are detected and encoded directly through the child's ongoing experiences. These signals provide information about the postnatal environment, particularly if the environment will be harsh and unpredictable (Del Giudice et al., 2011). A central assumption of the match -mismatch model is that the fetus regulation to different stimuli can result in a mismatch in which the neonate is poorly prepared for its environment.

Both theories agree that environmental changes during pregnancy directly affect the fetus's development by alerting different factors, including the DNA.

Although the availability of appropriate methodological tools has limited the study of human brain development and the effects of experiences on these processes, recent studies have begun to elucidate the connection between maternal stress and epigenetic changes in the fetus.

Most of the studies about long-term consequences of prenatal stress available now are in the animal model, even if a few studies in humans have been conducted. The literature indicates that prenatal exposures to certain forms of stress or maternal psychopathology translate into an increased risk for the child to develop behavior (O'Connor et al., 2003).

Several experiments have shown that the offspring of animals exposed to mild stress conditions during pregnancy are more vulnerable to stress response, primarily involving the hypothalamic-pituitary-adrenal (HPA). The activation of the HPA trigger stimulates the release of glucocorticoids (cortisol in humans and corticosterone in rodents), which can cross the placenta and induce changes in the DNA expression, translating into neurological and psychobiological changes associated with the experience of stress. In general, these studies confirmed that the short- and long-term effects of maternal stress can be traced to the offspring.

In a study by Cecil et al. (2016), neonates exposed to maternal stress (e.g., maternal psychopathology, criminal behaviors, substance use) in the prenatal period had higher DNA methylation levels of the oxytocin receptor gene compared to non-exposed neonates. Oxytocin is a hormone that plays a role in social bonding, reproduction, childbirth, and milk production (Dale, 1906). DNA methylation of the receptor gene results in a lower amount of the hormone in mothers exposed to trauma neonate.

Similarly, prenatal exposure to maternal depressive symptoms has been associated with the serotonergic SLC6A4 gene's altered methylation. This gene regulates the hormone serotonin, which, among many other biological functions, regulates mood, cognition, learning, memory, and numerous physiological processes.

A large study using a Canadian population in Quebec has been used to establish a relationship between trauma and epigenetic changes in humans. In January 1998, five days of freezing rain collapsed the power grid of southern Quebec, leaving three million people without electricity for as long as 45 days in the coldest month of the year. Five months after the ice storm, a group of researchers lead by King recruited 224 women who were pregnant during the crisis. These women received detailed questionnaires to assess their levels of objective hardship (threat, loss, scope, and change), their cognitive appraisal of the crisis (negative, neutral, positive), and their degree of subjective distress (post-traumatic stress symptoms), and also provided saliva samples over 24 hours to assess diurnal cortisol. Both maternal psychopathology and child development have been monitored through questionnaires beginning at six months postpartum and face-to-face assessments starting at two years. Detailed child assessments included cognitive, behavioral, motor, and many physical assessments such as cardiovascular function, HPA axis (cortisol awakening response, diurnal cortisol, stress reactivity), growth and metabolism, immune function, and more (King et al., 2012). This study's results have shown that in children of mothers exposed to stressful conditions, DNA methylation is much higher than in children conceived in the same period from mothers who were not exposed to stressful conditions during the pregnancy (Cao-Lei et al., 2014).

Epigenetics and Trauma in Infants and Young Children

Parental stress, reduced sensitivity of parents to infant cues, and childhood neglect/abuse may lead to a cascade of biological changes that compromise infants' functioning, leading to effects that persist into adolescence and adulthood. Moreover, genetic and environmental factors may heighten the vulnerability of infants to these effects. For the high-risk neonate, both underlying vulnerability and adverse early-life experiences are characteristics that may ultimately lead to divergent developmental pathways that compromise future health and well-being. Thus, understanding the ways in which parental care can alter infant development may provide insight into the potential interventions and practices that are critical in promoting healthy children, adolescents, and adults.

Laboratory studies of rodents suggest that adverse experiences occurring during infant development lead to brain architecture and function changes. These effects are particularly evident when the quality of the parent-infant interaction is affected, either through parental stress or by manipulating the quality and/or quantity of parental care toward infants. More recent approaches to the study of the influence of parental effects have determined that, in addition to physiologic and neurobiological outcomes, the quality of the parent-infant interactions may induce a molecular change in offspring, which alters the patterns of gene expression present in specific brain regions. These epigenetic effects indicate that the early-life environment's quality can change the activity of genes, thus illustrating the dynamic interplay between genes and environmental experiences in shaping development. For example, research in animals has shown that stressful experiences – where the pregnant mother is exposed or where the offspring is exposed soon after birth – produce epigenetic changes that chemically modify the receptor in the brain that controls the stress hormone cortisol and, therefore, determines the body's response to threat (the fight-or-flight response).

The literature on behavioral epigenetics in humans is smaller than the literature that has been written about epigenetics in animals. Despite fewer studies, data had confirmed similar findings in animals. For example, a survey of a group of maltreated preschool children ages 3–5 with higher levels of early adversity (such as bullying, physical and psychological maltreatments) were found to have an increase in DNA methylation in genes involved in stress response compared to children of the same age that were not maltreated (Moffitt and Klaus-Grawe Think, 2013).

A more comprehensive study has focused on the mother-infant dyad by analyzing behavior and the hormone levels of oxytocin (OXTRm) (Krol et al., 2019). Oxytocin (OXTR) is a crucial regulator of human social behavior (also known as the love and cuddling hormone). Increased amounts of OXTR have been also linked to a greater ability to cope with stress and an increase in social skills (Chaffin et al., 2011; Champagne and Curley, 2005). In addition, DNA methylation of OXTRm is associated with individual differences in adult and infant brain responses to social information (Krol et al., 2019).

Krol et al. were able to correlate the level of OXTRm in infants with the quality of maternal engagement. In addition, they tested the hypothesis that infant OXTRm levels at 18 months would be associated with their behavioral temperament, positing OXTRm as a promising epigenetic mark reflective of variability in early behavioral traits. For this study, 101 infants (and their mothers) were followed from 5 to 18 months of age. At 5 months, maternal and infant behavioral engagement was assessed during a free-play interaction. At 18 months, they examined infant behavioral temperament. On both occasions, OXTRm was measured in mothers and infants (Krol et al., 2019). Results showed that while OXTR levels changed from the 5- to 18-month visit in the infants, the hormone levels remained stable in the mother. The researchers also found that an increase in the quality of maternal engagement at 5 months translated into an increased expression of OXTR more than one year later. These results suggested that maternal engagement may have the potential to up-regulate the oxytocin system in human offspring.

The idea that a fetus and an infant are susceptible to the environment, which is mostly represented by the mother's relationship to them, is not a novel concept in psychology and psychoanalysis. Previous reports have established correlations between environmental conditions and changes in the DNA and gene expression. Thus, epigenetics has corroborated the psychoanalytic model in which experiences directly impact and change human behavior.

Psychotherapies and Epigenetics

Freud meant to develop psychoanalysis as a "natural science of psychology" based on quantifiable psychic processes. Freud was unsuccessful because he realized that words and meaning could not be reduced to molecular mechanisms and because he was far ahead of scientific knowledge of his time. The recent advances of scientific knowledge have made it possible to bridge the gap between "words" and "physiology." Epigenetic regulatory mechanisms have brought together the neurobiological mechanisms underlying mental functioning and the relationships between genes and the environment (Isles and Wilkinson, 2008). Thus, epigenetics serves as a molecular bridge between "nature" and "nurture" (Tammen et al., 2013). Another way to understand epigenetics using a psychoanalytic lens is to think about it as a biological key that allows the environmental conditions to be internalized and become part of a collection of processes, representations, and affects (mostly unconscious), which Freud referred to as "psychical reality."

One of an organism's hallmarks is the ability to respond to change in the environment by modifying patterns of behavior and learning from experience.

Kandel theorized that psychotherapies are a way of learning in response to environmental stimuli. Kandel wrote, "insofar as psychotherapy is successful in bringing about substantive changes in behavior, it does so by producing alterations in gene expression" (Kandel, 1998, p. 460). Jablonka and Lamb (Jaenisch and Bird, 2003) postulated that human transmission of information happens biologically or by behavior and by transmitting information through language. In their view, inheritance is a genetic, epigenetic, behavioral, and symbolic combination, with each part of that combination interacting with the others to form the phenotype. Stahl (2012) suggested that psychotherapy functions as an "epigenetic drug" capable of inducing epigenetic modifications by exercising its effects on neurobiological circuits, which are ultimately reflected on a clinical symptom level.

In the last few decades, it becomes clearer that mental illness origins are linked to the environment-genome interaction and that this interaction depends on epigenetic mechanisms (Heim and Binder, 2012). We are also more aware that psychotherapy's results depend primarily on non-specific factors related to interpersonal processes and that it produces biological changes in the central nervous system (Kraaijenvanger et al., 2020).

The interplay between psychotherapies and their effect on the DNA is a new investigation area, and only a few studies are available. Although studies in animal models cannot be used as an example to describe psychotherapies' ability to influence DNA, promising animal studies applying psychoenvironmental interventions have shown environmental enrichment to exert an effect on behavior (Schiele et al., 2020) at the neurobiological level (Laitinen, 1990). For example, animals with mental and neurodegenerative disorders exposed to enriched environments (increased social interaction, larger housing cases, toys, periodic stimulation, etc.) showed brain morphological changes, re-constituted learning behaviors, and access to long-term memories (Schiele et al., 2020).

Recently, researchers have been focusing on identifying specific genes that could predict therapy outcome (Lester and Eley, 2013). Yehuda et al. (2013) studied 16 veterans with PTSD and the effect of 12 weeks of psychotherapy on DNA methylation of the GR involved in stress response in humans. Methylation levels were measured from blood samples collected before and after psychotherapy. The veteran group was divided into responders and non-responders according to the presence or absence of PTSD criteria, measured through the Structured Clinical Interview for DSM-IV (SCID). Gene methylation predicted treatment response but did not change significantly over time. Patients who had higher methylation before treatment had a better response to intervention.

In a psychotherapy-epigenetic study, Ziegler et al. (2016) examined DNA changes in the monoamino oxidase A (MAOA), a gene involved in the essential hormones dopamine, norepinephrine, and serotonin. In this study, 28 patients with a panic disorder diagnosis and 28 healthy controls were treated with six CBT weeks. Blood samples from all individuals were collected before and after CBT treatment. Results showed a reduction of panic symptoms in subjects who undergo therapy, which correlates with an increase in DNA methylation in the MAOA gene compared to healthy controls (Ziegler et al., 2016).

In another study, 98 children with anxiety disorders were tested for an association between DNA methylation in the FKBP5 and GR (two genes involved in stress response in humans) and response to CBT. The percentage of DNA methylation at the FKBP5 and GR promoter regions was measured before and after 12 weeks of CBT. Change in FKBP5 and GR DNA methylation was significantly associated with treatment response. Participants who demonstrated the most significant reduction in anxiety also showed a decrease in DNA methylation during CBT treatment. Conversely, subjects with little/no reduction in anxiety showed an increase in DNA methylation (Roberts et al., 2015). Several other studies have supported this initial evidence associating psychotherapies with changes (Roberts et al., 2019; Schiele et al., 2020).

Unfortunately, no epigenetic research is available for more prolonged therapy, such as psychoanalysis. This research would involve a large cohort of patients who would have to be followed for a long time (years). Each patient would be required to provide biological samples every three to six months. These broad studies would require organization and capital, but would provide precious information that could be used in the therapeutic settings and at the social level.

The exploration of the epigenetic mechanisms that may underlie psychotherapeutic changes is just at the beginning. More studies are necessary with increasing sample sizes, homogenizing both phenotype and type of psychotherapy, including healthy controls, before researchers are able to establish a direct correlation between therapy and change in DNA conformation. Nevertheless, these initial studies indicate that selected genes and endocrinological modifications are subject to environmental regulation and that psychotherapy constitutes a form of "environmental regulation" that may alter the epigenetic state.

Clinical Implications

In focusing on the relationship between therapist and patient in the clinical setting, it is important to consider how a therapist may benefit from knowledge of epigenetics. I believe epigenetics offers a possibility for the analyst to validate and corroborate the theoretical and clinical relational position. The work that happens between analyst and patient, as seen through the lens of epigenetics, has the potential of effecting great change, in both mind and at the level of DNA.

Ferenczi first suggested that the therapist functions as a supportive, empathic witness in the effort to facilitate an environment in which the dissociative aspects of the patient could become available to the patient-therapist dyad. Epigenetics offers the analyst the possibility to link and bind together the Ferenczian tradition with the more recent theory of affect regulation postulated by Stern (1985) and others. The importance of affect regulation has been highlighted by many, and one of those who has emphasized its importance is the psychologist Allan Schore (1994), who has argued that the core sense of self results from patterns of affect regulation that are coordinated across different self-states, leading to a sense of cohesiveness of inner experience. Thus, it appears even more evident that the therapist functions as an external affect-regulative factor that mediates or facilitates self-regulation within a transference-countertransference field.

I have also found epigenetics useful in the consultation room. On more than one occasion, I have used epigenetic theory with patients claiming that their problems have a genetic component that cannot be altered. The purpose of such declarations by patients is to undermine the role of the therapy (and the therapist). It also absolves the patient of any responsibility and allows them to play a passive role in their own life. In many instances, I found that the ability to challenge patients' beliefs with data-based facts provokes a shift in the therapeutic relationship. I have also used epigenetic examples to validate patients' feelings about positive changes in their lives and their ability to break the narrowed and restricted repetitive patterns they felt confined to. The result is that the patient feels reassured, and the therapeutic relationship strengthens. Thus, epigenetic knowledge can be added to the arsenal at the therapist's disposal and find its place in the consultation room.

Conclusions

In this chapter, I introduced and discussed the new concept of epigenetics and presented scientific evidence supporting the notion that environmental conditions influence DNA expression changes. Additionally, I argued that recent research suggests a close connection between DNA and many aspects of psychoanalysis, particularly the healing of trauma. Research in epigenetics has helped clarify that psychological trauma triggers DNA changes, resulting in shifts in gene expression that directly impact the neurons in our brain, our memories, and our emotional behaviors. More importantly, researchers have found that epigenetic changes caused by psychological trauma can be transmitted from generation to generation, which validates the psychoanalytic concept of intergenerational transmission of trauma.

These new findings validate the importance of psychoanalytical treatment, which is more than just a collection of techniques for influencing human behavior. Still, now it extends into the realm of biological science. These new findings could redefine psychoanalysis as a therapeutic tool and a preventive instrument that could be used during the prenatal period of gestation and extended to settings such as schools and workplaces, aiming to prevent trauma instead of curing it.

Although psychoanalysis and epigenetics may seem very different, the more we learn about epigenetic mechanisms, the clearer it becomes that the fundamental mechanism that underlies and regulates the two disciplines transcend the barriers between them. Psychoanalysis and epigenetics validate each other and bring together the psyche, soma, environment, and constitution. Each discipline enriches the other.

References

Barker, D. J., Osmond, C., Golding, J., Kuh, D. & Wadsworth, M. E. (1989). Growth in utero, blood pressure in childhood and adult life, and mortality from cardiovascular disease. *BMJ*, 298, 564–567.

Bion, W. R. (1962). The psycho-analytic study of thinking. A theor of thinking. *The International Journal of Psycho-Analysis*, 43, 306–310.

Bock, J., Poeschel, J., Schindler, J., Borner, F., Shachar-Dadon, A., et al. 2016. Transgenerational sex-specific impact of preconception stress on the development of dendritic spines and dendritic length in the medial prefrontal cortex. *Brain Structure and Function*, 221, 855–863.

Bohacek, J., Engmann, O., Germain, P. L., Schelbert, S. & Mansuy, I. M. (2018). Transgenerational epigenetic inheritance: From biology to society-Summary Latsis Symposium Aug 28–30, 2017, Zurich, Switzerland. *Environmental Epigenetics*, 4, dvy012.

Boschan, P. J. (2008). Childhood and trauma. *The American Journal of Psychoanalysis*, 68, 24–32.

Bowlby, J. (1958). The nature of the child's tie to his mother. *The International Journal of Psycho-Analysis*, 39, 350–373.

Braun, P. R., Tanaka-Sahker, M., Chan, A. C., Jellison, S. S., Klisares, M. J., et al. (2019). Genome-wide DNA methylation investigation of glucocorticoid exposure within buccal samples. *Psychiatry and Clinical Neurosciences*, 73, 323–330.

Breuer, J. and Freud, S. (1893-1895). Studies on Hysteria. In Strachey, J. (ed. & Trans.), *The Standard Edition of the Complete Works of Sigmund Freud* (Vol. 2 pp. 1–335). London: Hogarth Press.

Caldji, C., Tannenbaum, B., Sharma, S., Francis, D., Plotsky, P. M. & Meaney, M. J. (1998). Maternal care during infancy regulates the development of neural systems mediating the expression of fearfulness in the rat. *Proceedings of the National Academy of Sciences of the United States of America*, 95, 5335–5340.

Cao-Lei, L., Massart, R., Suderman, M. J., Machnes, Z., Elgbeili, G., et al. (2014). DNA methylation signatures triggered by prenatal maternal stress exposure to a natural disaster: Project Ice Storm. *PLoS One*, 9, e107653.

Cecil, C. A., Walton, E., Smith, R. G., Viding, E., McCrory, E. J., et al. (2016). DNA methylation and substance-use risk: A prospective, genome-wide study spanning gestation to adolescence. *Translational Psychiatry*, 6, e976.

Chaffin, M., Funderburk, B., Bard, D., Valle, L. A. & Gurwitch, R. (2011). A combined motivation and parent-child interaction therapy package reduces child welfare recidivism in a randomized dismantling field trial. *Journal of Consulting and Clinical Psychology*, 79, 84–95.

Champagne, F. A. & Curley, J. P. (2005). How social experiences influence the brain. *Current Opinion in Neurobiology*, 15, 704–709.

Chan, J. C., Nugent, B. M. & Bale, T. L. (2018). Parental advisory: Maternal and paternal stress can impact offspring neurodevelopment. *Biological Psychiatry*, 83, 886–894.

Chaudoye, G., Strauss-Kahn, M. & Zebdi, R. (2017). Memory: Between traumatic shock and psychic historicization. *The International Journal of Psycho-Analysis*, 98, 985–997.

Collins, F. (2010). Has the revolution arrived? *Nature*, 464, 674–675.

Conradt, E., Lester, B. M., Appleton, A. A., Armstrong, D. A. & Marsit, C. J. (2013). The roles of DNA methylation of NR3C1 and 11beta-HSD2 and exposure to maternal mood disorder in utero on newborn neurobehavior. *Epigenetics*, 8, 1321–1329.

Cubas, P., Vincent, C. & Coen, E. (1999). An epigenetic mutation responsible for natural variation in floral symmetry. *Nature*, 401, 157–161.

Dale, H. H. (1906). On some physiological actions of ergot. *The Journal of Physiology*, 34, 163–206.

De Bellis, M. D. & Zisk, A. (2014). The biological effects of childhood trauma. *Child and Adolescent Psychiatric Clinics of North America*, 23, 185–222, vii.

Del Giudice, M., Ellis, B. J. & Shirtcliff, E. A. (2011). The adaptive calibration model of stress responsivity. *Neuroscience and Biobehavioral Reviews*, 35, 1562–1592.

Dickson, D. A., Paulus, J. K., Mensah, V., Lem, J., Saavedra-Rodriguez, L., et al. (2018). Reduced levels of miRNAs 449 and 34 in sperm of mice and men exposed to early life stress. *Translational Psychiatry*, 8, 101.

Dunn, A. J. & Berridge, C. W. (1990). Physiological and behavioral responses to corticotropin-releasing factor administration: Is CRF a mediator of anxiety or stress responses? *Brain Research Reviews*, 15, 71–100.

Dunn, E. C., Soare, T. W., Zhu, Y., Simpkin, A. J., Suderman, M. J., et al. (2019). Sensitive periods for the effect of childhood adversity on DNA methylation: Results from a prospective, longitudinal study. *Biological Psychiatry*, 85, 838–849.

Egliston, K. A., McMahon, C. & Austin, M. P. (2007). Stress in pregnancy and infant HPA axis function: Conceptual and methodological issues relating to the use of salivary cortisol as an outcome measure. *Psychoneuroendocrinology*, 32, 1–13.

Ferenczi, S. (1955). *Confusion of the Tongues Between the Adults and the Child* (pp. 156–167). London: Hogarth Press.

Ferenczi, S. (1988). *The Clinical Diary of Sandor Ferenczi*. London: Harvard University Press.

Fernandez Arias, P., Yoshida, K., Brockington, I. F., Kernreiter, J. & Klier, C. M. (2019). Foetal abuse. *Archives of Women's Mental Health*, 22, 569–573.

Finegood, E. D., Raver, C. C., DeJoseph, M. L. & Blair, C. (2017). Parenting in poverty: Attention bias and anxiety interact to predict parents' perceptions of daily parenting hassles. *Journal of Family Psychology*, 31, 51–60.

Fonagy, P. (1999). The transgenerational transmission of holocaust trauma. Lessons learned from the analysis of an adolescent with obsessive-compulsive disorder. *Attachment & Human Development*, 1, 92–114.

Francis, D., Diorio, J., Liu, D. & Meaney, M. J. (1999). Nongenomic transmission across generations of maternal behavior and stress responses in the rat. *Science*, 286, 1155–1158.

Francis, R. C. (2011). *Epigenetics. How Environment Shapes Our Genes*. New York: Norton.

Freud, S. (1892). *Preface and Footnotes of Charcot's Tuesday Lectures*. In Strachey, J. (ed. & Trans.), *The Standard Edition of the Complete Psychological Works of Sigmund Freud* (Vol. 1, pp. 131–143). London: Hogarth Press.

———. (1920). *Beyond the Pleasure Principle*. London, Vienna: The International Psycho-Analytical Press, MCMXII [1922].

———. (1923). The ego and the id. In Strachey, J. (ed. & Trans.), *The Standard Edition of the Complete Psychological Works of Sigmund Freud* (Vol. 19, pp. 1–66). London: Hogarth Press.

Gapp, K., Bohacek, J., Grossmann, J., Brunner, A. M., Manuella, F., et al. (2016). Potential of environmental enrichment to prevent transgenerational effects of paternal trauma. *Neuropsychopharmacology*, 41, 2749–2758.

Goldberg, A. D., Allis, C. D. & Bernstein, E. (2007). Epigenetics: A landscape takes shape. *Cell*, 128, 635–638.

Halfmann, R., Jarosz, D. F., Jones, S. K., Chang, A., Lancaster, A. K. & Lindquist, S. 2012. Prions are a common mechanism for phenotypic inheritance in wild yeasts. *Nature*, 482, 363–368.

Harker, A., Raza, S., Williamson, K., Kolb, B. & Gibb, R. (2015). Preconception paternal stress in rats alters dendritic morphology and connectivity in the brain of developing male and female offspring. *Neuroscience*, 303, 200–210.

Heard, E. & Martienssen, R. A. (2014). Transgenerational epigenetic inheritance: Myths and mechanisms. *Cell*, 157, 95–109.

Heim, C. & Binder, E. B. (2012). Current research trends in early life stress and depression: Review of human studies on sensitive periods, gene-environment interactions, and epigenetics. *Experimental Neurology*, 233, 102–111.

Herringa, R. J., Phillips, M. L., Fournier, J. C., Kronhaus, D. M. & Germain, A. (2013). Childhood and adult trauma both correlate with dorsal anterior cingulate activation to threat in combat veterans. *Psychological Medicine*, 43, 1533–1542.

Hutchinson, K. M., McLaughlin, K. J., Wright, R. L., Bryce Ortiz, J., Anouti, D. P., et al. (2012). Environmental enrichment protects against the effects of chronic stress on cognitive and morphological measures of hippocampal integrity. *Neurobiology of Learning and Memory*, 97, 250–260.

Isles, A. R. & Wilkinson, L. S. (2008). Epigenetics: What is it and why is it important to mental disease? *British Medical Bulletin*, 85, 35–45.

Iyengar, U., Kim, S., Martinez, S., Fonagy, P. & Strathearn, L. (2014). Unresolved trauma in mothers: Intergenerational effects and the role of reorganization. *Frontiers in Psychology*, 5, 966.

Jackowski, A. P., de Araujo, C. M., de Lacerda, A. L., Mari Jde, J. & Kaufman, J. (2009). Neurostructural imaging findings in children with post-traumatic stress disorder: Brief review. *Psychiatry and Clinical Neurosciences*, 63, 1–8.

Jacobson, L. & Sapolsky, R. (1991). The role of the hippocampus in feedback regulation of the hypothalamic-pituitary-adrenocortical axis. *Endocrine Reviews*, 12, 118–134.

Jaenisch, R. & Bird, A. (2003). Epigenetic regulation of gene expression: How the genome integrates intrinsic and environmental signals. *Nature Genetics*, 33 Suppl, 245–254.

Jaroff, L. (1989). The gene hunt. *Time*, 133, 62–67.

John, R. M. (2019). Prenatal adversity modulates the quality of maternal care via the exposed offspring. *BioEssays: News and Reviews in Molecular, Cellular and Developmental Biology*, 41, e1900025.

Jordan, D., Kuehn, S., Katifori, E. & Leibler, S. (2013). Behavioral diversity in microbes and low-dimensional phenotypic spaces. *Proceedings of the National Academy of Sciences of the United States of America*, 110, 14018–14023.

Kader, F., Ghai, M. & Maharaj, L. (2018). The effects of DNA methylation on human psychology. *Behavioural Brain Research*, 346, 47–65.

Kandel, E. R. (1998). A new intellectual framework for psychiatry. *The American Journal of Psychiatry*, 155, 457–469.

Kaur, P., Shorey, L. E., Ho, E., Dashwood, R. H. & Williams, D. E. (2013). The epigenome as a potential mediator of cancer and disease prevention in prenatal development. *Nutrition Reviews*, 71, 441–457.

Keller, E. F. (2000). *The Century of the Gene*. Cambridge, MA and London: Harvard University Press.

Khan, M. M. (1963). The concept of cumulative Trauma. *The Psychoanalytic Study of the Child*, 18, 286–306.

King, S., Dancause, K., Turcotte-Tremblay, A. M., Veru, F. & Laplante, D. P. (2012). Using natural disasters to study the effects of prenatal maternal stress on child health and development. *Birth Defects Research. Part C, Embryo Today: Reviews*, 96, 273–288.

Klein, M. (1946). Notes on some schizoid mechanisms. *The International Journal of Psycho-Analysis*, 27, 99–110.

Kraaijenvanger, E. J., Pollok, T. M., Monninger, M., Kaiser, A., Brandeis, D., et al. (2020). Impact of early life adversities on human brain functioning: A coordinate-based meta-analysis. *Neuroscience and Biobehavioral Reviews*, 113, 62–76.

Krol, K. M., Moulder, R. G., Lillard, T. S., Grossmann, T. & Connelly, J. J. (2019). Epigenetic dynamics in infancy and the impact of maternal engagement. *Science Advances*, 5(10).

Lacan, J. (1968). *The Language of the Self: The Function of Language in Psychoanalysis*. London: The Johns Hopkins Press.

Laitinen, L. V. (1990). Loss of motivation for speaking with bilateral lacunes in the anterior limb of the internal capsule. *Clinical Neurology and Neurosurgery*, 92, 177–178.

Lam, L. L., Emberly, E., Fraser, H. B., Neumann, S. M., Chen, E., et al. (2012). Factors underlying variable DNA methylation in a human community cohort. *Proceedings of the National Academy of Sciences of the United States of America*, 109, Suppl 2, 17253–17260.

Lester, K. J. & Eley, T. C. (2013). Therapygenetics: Using genetic markers to predict response to psychological treatment for mood and anxiety disorders. *Biology of Mood & Anxiety Disorders*, 3, 4.

Liu, D., Diorio, J., Tannenbaum, B., Caldji, C., Francis, D., et al. (1997). Maternal care, hippocampal glucocorticoid receptors, and hypothalamic-pituitary-adrenal responses to stress. *Science*, 277, 1659–1662.

Logue, M. W., Miller, M. W., Wolf, E. J., Huber, B. R., Morrison, F. G., et al. (2020). An epigenome-wide association study of posttraumatic stress disorder in US veterans implicates several new DNA methylation loci. *Clinical Epigenetics*, 12, 46.

Massie, H. & Szajnberg, N. (2006). My life is a longing: Child abuse and its adult sequelae. Results of the Brody longitudinal study from birth to age 30. *The International Journal of Psycho-Analysis*, 87, 471–496.

McArdle, H. J., Andersen, H. S., Jones, H. & Gambling, L. (2006). Fetal programming: Causes and consequences as revealed by studies of dietary manipulation in rats – a review. *Placenta*, 27, Suppl A, S56–S60.

McGowan, P. O., Sasaki, A., D'Alessio, A. C., Dymov, S., Labonte, B., et al. (2009). Epigenetic regulation of the glucocorticoid receptor in human brain associates with childhood abuse. *Nature Neuroscience*, 12, 342–348.

Moffitt, T. E., Klaus-Grawe Think, T. (2013). Childhood exposure to violence and lifelong health: Clinical intervention science and stress-biology research join forces. *Development and Psychopathology*, 25, 1619–1634.

Mucci, C. (2014). Trauma, healing and the reconstruction of truth. *The American Journal of Psychoanalysis*, 74, 31–47.

Nederhof, E. & Schmidt, M. V. (2012). Mismatch or cumulative stress: Toward an integrated hypothesis of programming effects. *Physiology & Behavior*, 106, 691–700.

Nicoletto, S. F. & Rinaldi, A. (2011). In the womb's shadow. The theory of prenatal programming as the fetal origin of various adult diseases is increasingly supported by a wealth of evidence. *EMBO Reports*, 12, 30–34.

O'Connor, T. G., Heron, J., Golding, J., Glover, V. & Team, A. S. (2003). Maternal antenatal anxiety and behavioural/emotional problems in children: A test of a programming hypothesis. *Journal of Child Psychology and Psychiatry, and Allied Disciplines*, 44, 1025–1036.

Ohlstein, E. H., Horohonich, S., Shebuski, R. J. & Ruffolo, R. R., Jr. (1989). Localization and characterization of alpha-2 adrenoceptors in the isolated canine pulmonary vein. *The Journal of Pharmacology and Experimental Therapeutics*, 248, 233–239.

Perroud, N., Rutembesa, E., Paoloni-Giacobino, A., Mutabaruka, J., Mutesa, L., et al. (2014). The Tutsi genocide and transgenerational transmission of maternal stress: Epigenetics and biology of the HPA axis. *The World Journal of Biological Psychiatry: The Official Journal of the World Federation of Societies of Biological Psychiatry*, 15, 334–345.

Peschansky, V. J. & Wahlestedt, C. (2014). Non-coding RNAs as direct and indirect modulators of epigenetic regulation. *Epigenetics*, 9, 3–12.

Provenzi, L., Brambilla, M., Scotto di Minico, G., Montirosso, R. & Borgatti, R. (2019). Maternal caregiving and DNA methylation in human infants and children: Systematic review. *Genes, Brain and Behavior*, e12616.

Ptashne, M. (2007). On speaking, writing and inspiration. *Current Biology: CB*, 17, R348–R349.

Roberts, S., Keers, R., Breen, G., Coleman, J. R. I., Johren, P., et al. (2019). DNA methylation of FKBP5 and response to exposure-based psychological therapy. *American Journal of Medical Genetics. Part B, Neuropsychiatric Genetics: The Official Publication of the International Society of Psychiatric Genetics*, 180, 150–158.

Roberts, S., Keers, R., Lester, K. J., Coleman, J. R., Breen, G., et al. (2015). HPA axis related genes and response to psychological therapies: Genetics and epigenetics. *Depression and Anxiety*, 32, 861–870.

Sanz, J., Maurizio, P. L., Snyder-Mackler, N., Simons, N. D., Voyles, T., et al. (2020). Social history and exposure to pathogen signals modulate social status effects on gene regulation in rhesus macaques. *Proceedings of the National Academy of Sciences of the United States of America*, 117, 23317–23322.

Schiele, M. A., Gottschalk, M. G. & Domschke, K. (2020). The applied implications of epigenetics in anxiety, affective and stress-related disorders – A review and synthesis on psychosocial stress, psychotherapy and prevention. *Clinical Psychology Review*, 77, 101830.

Schore, A. N. (1994). *Affect Regulation and the Origin of the Self. The Neurobiology of Emotional Development*. Hillsdale, NJ: Lawrence Erlbaum Associates.

———. (2009). Relational trauma and the developing right brain: An interface of psychoanalytic self psychology and neuroscience. *Annals of the New York Academy of Sciences*, 1159, 189–203.

Sharma, U., Conine, C. C., Shea, J. M., Boskovic, A., Derr, A. G., et al. (2016). Biogenesis and function of tRNA fragments during sperm maturation and fertilization in mammals. *Science*, 351, 391–396.

Shin, L. M., Rauch, S. L. & Pitman, R. K. (2006). Amygdala, medial prefrontal cortex, and hippocampal function in PTSD. *Annals of the New York Academy of Sciences*, 1071, 67–79.

Shonkoff, J. P., Garner, A. S., Committee on Psychosocial Aspects of Child and Family Health; Committee on Early Childhood Adoption, and Dependent Care; Session on Developmental and Behavioral Pediatrics. (2012). The lifelong effects of early childhood adversity and toxic stress. *Pediatrics*, 129, e232–e246.

Siebold, C. (2013). Trauma and the complexity of internal and external experience: A brief review. *Psychoanalytic Social Work*, 20, 76–86.

Stahl, S. M. (2012). Psychotherapy as an epigenetic 'drug': Psychiatric therapeutics target symptoms linked to malfunctioning brain circuits with psychotherapy as well as with drugs. *Journal of Clinical Pharmacy and Therapeutics*, 37, 249–253.

Stern, D. (1985). *The Inter Personal World of the Infant*. New York: Basic Books.

Tammen, S. A., Friso, S. & Choi, S. W. (2013). Epigenetics: The link between nature and nurture. *Molecular Aspects of Medicine*, 34, 753–764.

Turecki, G. & Meaney, M. J. (2016). Effects of the social environment and stress on glucocorticoid receptor gene methylation: A systematic review. *Biological Psychiatry*, 79, 87–96.

van der Kolk, B. (2000). Posttraumatic stress disorder and the nature of trauma. *Dialogues in Clinical Neuroscience*, 2, 7–22.

Walton, E., Hass, J., Liu, J., Roffman, J. L., Bernardoni, F., et al. (2016). Correspondence of DNA methylation between blood and brain tissue and its application to schizophrenia research. *Schizophrenia Bulletin*, 42, 406–414.

Weaver, I. C., Cervoni, N., Champagne, F. A., D'Alessio, A. C., Sharma, S., et al. (2004). Epigenetic programming by maternal behavior. *Nature Neuroscience*, 7, 847–854.

Wolffe, A. P. & Matzke, M. A. (1999). Epigenetics: Regulation through repression. *Science*, 286, 481–486.

Wu, J., Bao, J., Kim, M., Yuan, S., Tang, C., et al. (2014). Two miRNA clusters, miR-34b/c and miR-449, are essential for normal brain development, motile ciliogenesis, and spermatogenesis. *Proceedings of the National Academy of Sciences of the United States of America*, 111, E2851–E2857.

Yehuda, R., Daskalakis, N. P., Bierer, L. M., Bader, H. N., Klengel, T., et al. (2016). Holocaust exposure induced intergenerational effects on FKBP5 methylation. *Biological Psychiatry*, 80, 372–380.

Yehuda, R., Daskalakis, N. P., Desarnaud, F., Makotkine, I., Lehrner, A. L., et al. (2013). Epigenetic biomarkers as predictors and correlates of symptom improvement following psychotherapy in combat veterans with PTSD. *Frontiers in Psychiatry*, 4, 118.

Yehuda, R., Pratchett, L. C., Elmes, M. W., Lehrner, A., Daskalakis, N. P., et al. (2014). Glucocorticoid-related predictors and correlates of post-traumatic stress disorder treatment response in combat veterans. *Interface Focus*, 4, 20140048.

Ziegler, C., Richter, J., Mahr, M., Gajewska, A., Schiele, M. A., et al. (2016). MAOA gene hypomethylation in panic disorder-reversibility of an epigenetic risk pattern by psychotherapy. *Translational Psychiatry*, 6, e773.

Part 4

Neuropsychoanalysis

Chapter 6

Neuropsychoanalysis
What, How, and Why

John Dall'Aglio

What Sort of (Neuro)science? What Sort of Psychoanalysis?

A longstanding question for psychoanalysis has been *is psychoanalysis a science?* Although psychoanalysis boasts considerable scientific support for its basic concepts and as a clinical practice (Shedler, 2010), should one simply place psychoanalysis in the lineup of modern sciences? Is there not something different about psychoanalysis as a *science of the subject*?

Regarding this question, an important inversion is *what sort of science could include psychoanalysis?* (Lacan, 1964; Laurent, 1995). Questioning *what sort of science* . . . opens a helpful space to *rethink* science. Critics of (dialogue with) natural science warn against a (bio)reductive elimination of subjective meaning-making (Blass and Carmeli, 2007). Nevertheless, an eye critical of bio-reductionism should not swing its gaze to the opposite extreme of 'mental' reductionism or isolationism (Sandberg, 2019). Such a turn risks making the mind somehow separate from the rest of nature.

Thus, I claim, an additional inversion is needed: *what sort of psychoanalysis could include science?* Linking psychoanalysis with the natural sciences necessitates rethinking *both* psychoanalysis and science. What sort of psychoanalysis could critically integrate natural science while avoiding both the Charybdis of reductionism and the Scylla of rejectionism?

I claim that neuropsychoanalysis can be one answer to these questions. Neuropsychoanalysis is, first and foremost, a *dialogue* – a bi-directional practice which generates new concepts and possibilities between and within psychoanalysis and the neurosciences. This chapter discusses my views[1] on neuropsychoanalysis. Rather than attempt to give an exhaustive review of the field, I will illustrate how the benefits of neuropsychoanalysis can be indexed to its dialogic structure. My discussion will thereby

DOI: 10.4324/9781003271499-11

focus on the elementary coordinates which give neuropsychoanalysis its enriching capacity.

What Is Neuropsychoanalysis? Dialectics of the Mental Apparatus

Before proceeding, it is worthwhile to ask *why neuroscience?* What makes neuroscience different from other disciplines like art, philosophy, literature, or cultural studies? These other fields have certainly been fruitful interlocutors for psychoanalysis. Given the contemporary predominance of biomedical psychiatry, the neuroscientific turn might be criticized as 'getting with the trends.' I do not suggest that knowledge from these other disciplines is inferior to neuroscience – in many cases, such disciplines shed humanizing light upon neurological and psychic processes. I claim that the importance of neuroscience is not epistemological superiority, but its unique *position* relative to psychoanalysis.

Dual-Aspect Monism: The Philosophical Basis of Neuropsychoanalysis

The neurosciences (i.e., the many sciences of the brain) hold this unique position because neuroscience is an objective perspective on the same *thing-in-nature* that psychoanalysis studies from the subjective perspective. This philosophical position is called 'dual-aspect monism' (see Figure 6.1). There is a single *thing-in-nature* (monism; Freud called this *thing* the 'mental apparatus'), yet there exist two (dual) radically different lenses (aspects) to view it (Solms, 2015).

Decades of neuropsychological studies testify to the link between brain and mind. Survivors of brain lesions are often profoundly impaired on certain mental functions and in some cases completely change personalities. To give one example, Zúñiga (2017) reports a case of a patient with damage to the orbitofrontal cortex due to a ruptured aneurysm. Neurologically, the orbitofrontal cortex has a central role in regulating powerful affective impulses. This patient developed impulsive, reactive, and ego-dystonic outbursts of violent rage. Zúñiga notes that interpersonal incidents – often involving women – commonly preceded these outbursts. Despite the impulsivity, the patient experienced heavy guilt, indicating some integrity of awareness and moral responsibility. A template of these outbursts (and guilt) could be traced to early experiences with the patient's mother

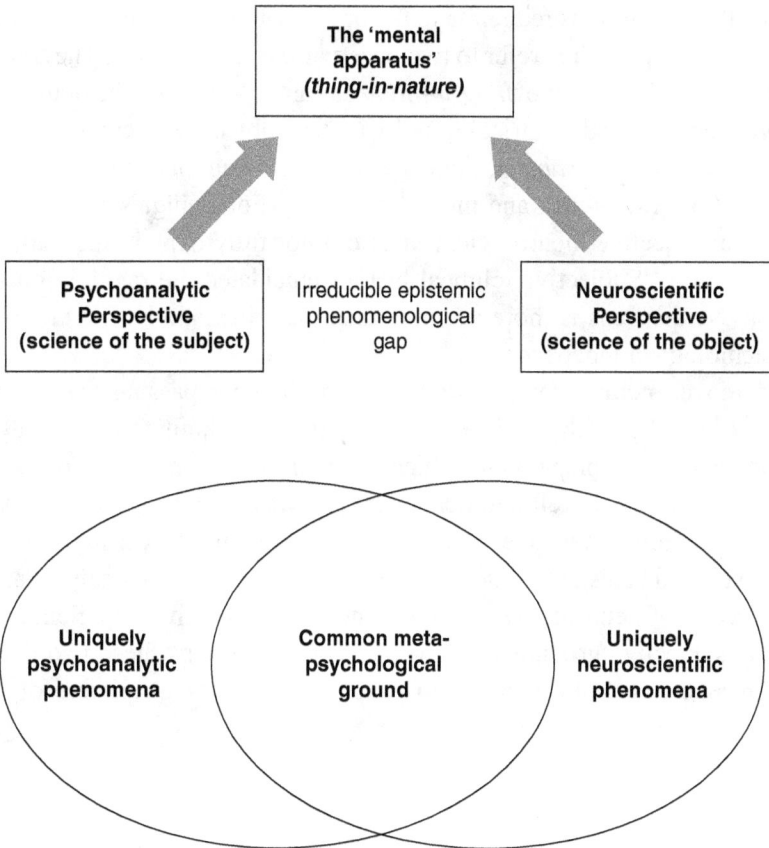

Figure 6.1 Visual depiction of dual-aspect monism. Top panel: there exists a single *thing-in-nature* with two observational perspectives, the subjective lens (psychoanalysis) and the objective lens (neuroscience). Bottom panel: neuropsychoanalysis involves (1) bridging theories and data from these lenses to inform common meta-psychology and (2) maintaining the space of phenomena which are unique to each perspective, due to the 'epistemic, phenomenological gap' between the two lenses.

and their ongoing relational ambivalence. Thus, while something of the personality remained intact, the brain injury caused substantial behavioral and personality change – namely, impulsive rage – which was experienced as external to the ego. Such cases are only one line of evidence (with developmental and brain imaging methods being some others) supporting the notion that our psychical being is dependent upon the integrity of our neurophysiological substrate (Kaplan-Solms and Solms, 2002).

Some clarifying points are in order. Firstly, dual-aspect monism does not imply that the mind is reducible to the brain. 'Objective' is not 'more real' than 'subjective' – they refer to two observational standpoints. The 'objective' view looks upon the *thing-in-nature* as an *object* called the brain, with neurochemicals and electrical impulses. The 'subjective' view looks upon the same *thing* as a *subject*, the experience of *being* that *thing-in-nature*, with feelings, thoughts, and mental dynamics. For Zúñiga's patient, note that the 'objective' neurological facts did not fully explain the patient's presentation. 'Subjective' clinical history elucidated the rageful constellation. Neither lens is more accurate than the other, and both retain their epistemological independence.

Moreover, neither perspective paints an all-encompassing view of the *thing-in-nature*. Each has its own epistemological limitations. There are some (aspects of) phenomena which are restricted to one lens. For example, no matter how well neurochemical pathways are described, the neuroscientist cannot describe what it is like to *feel* an affect using a purely neuroscientific epistemological frame. Likewise, the psychoanalyst has no knowledge of neurobiological underpinnings of affective experiences on purely subjective grounds. Neuropsychoanalysis brings these two disparate perspectives into dialogue to paint a more thorough picture of this *thing-in-nature*.

Dynamic Localization

One of the aims of neuropsychoanalytic dialogue is sketching out a common meta-psychological ground (Figure 6.1). If neuroscience and psychoanalysis are two views of the same *thing-in-nature*, then there must be certain common 'laws' which govern this *thing-in-nature*. Common meta-(neuro)psychology seeks to describe the laws which govern phenomena from both the subjective and objective lenses (Solms, 2021).

Importantly, this does not imply that one will find total parallel organizations between brain and mind. Rather, neuropsychoanalysis employs the lens of 'dynamic localization' (in the tradition of the Russian neuropsychologist Alexander Luria). Simply put, there is no one-to-one association between a neural area and a psychic process. Rather, psychic processes correspond to constellations of activity across various neural centers. A single neural center participates in *multiple* psychological processes (Solms, 2015). There will therefore be certain 'nodal points' between neural and psychic organizations, rather than a clean correspondence (Bazan and Detandt, 2015).

Recall Zúñiga's orbitofrontal patient. When viewed objectively, one area is damaged. In the psychical sphere, however, a range of functions are distorted: affective impulsivity, decision-making, and so on. Moreover, there was no general disinhibition of affective impulses (e.g., the patient was not hypersexual) – aggression was the primary issue. The differential organizations of mind and brain are an effect of the objective and subjective perspectives upon the *thing-in-nature*. From this diversity, one can infer the underlying mechanism(s) involved at a meta-psychological level (Zúñiga suggests a fracturing of the ego's boundary with the id, an absence of repression specific to aggression). Neuropsychoanalytic meta-psychology bridges 'objective' and 'subjective' phenomena, allowing some mapping of the brain.

This leads to another important clarification: neuropsychoanalysis is not a 'new school' of psychoanalysis. It is a dialogue in which different analytic schools 'refract,' depending on the meta-psychological lens(es) used to map phenomena. One may thus have Freudian, Kleinian, Lacanian, Kohutian, relational (and so on) neuropsychoanaly*ses* (Salas et al., 2021). As discussed later, neuropsychoanalysis opens a space for bringing these different schools together in a novel fashion.

Neuropsychoanalysis as a Frontier-Discipline

I wish to emphasize that neuropsychoanalytic meta-psychology ought not seek to resolve the objective-subjective gap but to straddle it. This bridge/ gap structure can be elucidated by characterizing neuropsychoanalysis as a 'frontier-discipline,' adopting Freud's (1915) notion of drive as a 'frontier-concept' (Johnston, 2005). For Freud, drive is a concept on the *border* between the mental and the somatic. The body is the 'frontier' of psychoanalysis, insofar as the body is meaningless in itself and must be indirectly inferred. The mind is the 'frontier' of neuroscience insofar as mechanistic accounts struggle to satisfyingly explain subjectivity. Drive encompasses *both* body and mind; it is a psychoanalytic concept which itself straddles a certain limit without resolving it. Indeed, the very non-resolution of drive (between bodily demand and mental work, insofar as drive never ceases its demand) generates the motor for psychical life.

Taking this framework as inspiration, I suggest thinking about neuropsychoanalysis analogously. Neuropsychoanalytic dialogue does not seek to *resolve* the gap between brain and mind. A meta-neuropsychological *lingua franca* (Kessler and Kessler, 2019) or bilingualism (Sandberg, 2019) does not imply an overcoming of what is 'lost in translation.' Rather, meta-neuropsychology seeks to better characterize this frontier, the points of connection *and disjuncture*. I will return to this point in the final section.

Reflecting on Freud's (1895) *Project for a Scientific Psychology*, one might add that this tension was one of the generators of psychoanalysis. Regardless of *why* Freud abandoned the *Project*, the fact remains that the concepts developed therein 'haunt' his entire corpus. Consider how many of Freud's works contain Strachey's footnotes referencing the *Project*. The tension of attempting to bridge brain and mind via meta-psychology is not a novel introduction by neuropsychoanalysis – it is one of the (repressed?) ancestors of psychoanalysis. Psychoanalysis has always been a frontier-discipline. In this sense, neuropsychoanalysis reinvigorates some basic coordinates of the field.

How Can One Go About Neuropsychoanalysis? Speaking Between Worlds

The Epistemological Challenge

Although one can propose a meta-neuropsychological framework for linking psychoanalysis and neuroscience, it remains questionable *how* neuroscience can enrich psychoanalysis. Blass and Carmeli (2007) emphasize that neuroscience does not discover any psychological phenomena (e.g., an attachment need). Such phenomena are (already) observed and described psychologically. Neuroscience only identifies *biological correlates* of psychological phenomena and therefore does not enrich the *psychological* meaningfulness of these phenomena already observed at a psychological level. For likeminded critics, the epistemic gap (cf. Figure 6.1) is too great.

A Threefold Movement of Neuropsychoanalytic Dialogue

Here, I wish to make explicit a proposal for navigating this epistemologi-cal challenge which I sketched out elsewhere (Dall'Aglio, 2021b). I call it a 'threefold movement.' First, one can map the brain using psychoanalytic meta-psychology. Importantly, such mapping should be done with careful attention to precise clinical and neuroscientific detail. One should be wary of rushed, superficial linkages (Fisher, 2020), yet, with careful work, bridges can be built.

After such meta-psychological mapping, in a second movement, one can observe the relationships among concepts in neural space. Because of the differential organizational perspectives (cf. dual-aspect monism and dynamic localization), the relationships in neural space will likely be very different or include new concepts from neighboring disciplines. In a third movement, one can then return to the psychoanalytic space to *consider what possibilities emerge* when evaluating these conceptual relationships. Meaning remains in psychoanalytic space and is therefore not reduced to biological epistemology – neuroscience contributes new *possible* (not determinate) relationships that participate in this meaning. This is not the only way to go about neuropsychoanalysis, but I find it helpful for explicitly addressing criticisms of bio-reductionism.

To give an example of this threefold movement, consider the debate regarding (classical Freudian) drives versus relational needs (Greenberg and Mitchell, 1983). While contemporary psychoanalytic developments have made fruitful use of a drive versus relational dichotomy, neuropsychoanalysis adds a nuancing lens to this issue.

When these concepts are mapped to functional neuroanatomy (first movement), one finds multiple bodily drives, such as hunger and thirst, but also emotional drives like FEAR, RAGE, PANIC, SEEKING, LUST, CARE, and PLAY[2] (Panksepp, 1998). Bodily drives have their roots in physiological need-states of the internal milieu. On the other hand, emotional drives are rooted in the brain itself, carrying predictions for socio-emotional states which are evolutionarily 'good,' such as nurturing young kin (CARE) or eliminating obstacles to the organism's goals (RAGE). While socio-relational *cognition* relies on the neocortex, basic relational *motives* arise from these emotional circuits. These systems function as drives insofar as deviations from their homeostatic 'set-points' generate unpleasure, and returning to these set-points generates pleasure. For example, under threat, FEAR generates fearful anxiety, along with a freeze/flight response. Loss of an attachment-object causes PANIC to generate a distinct separation-anxiety, with a 'protest-phase' seeking out the lost other. PLAY motivates 'as-if' explorations and joyful social interactions with others (e.g., rough-and-tumble play), facilitating social group-formations.

Blechner (2018) points out that relational needs (typically kept distinct from bodily drives) are, for Panksepp (1998), firmly rooted in biology. All of Panksepp's emotional drives imply a certain object-oriented stance (Solms, 2021). Thereby, 'drive' and 'relational need' converge in neural space (the second movement). Some drives *are* relational. In the psychoanalytic space, the question of a 'relational drive' emerges (the third movement). One can explore 'how these powerful, biologically based motivators shape relational configurations, as well as how relational configurations shape the expression of these motivators' (Blechner, 2018, p. 676).

Given the dialogic structure of neuropsychoanalysis, one can reverse this threefold formula. That is, psychoanalytic space can be mapped with neural concepts. Relationships among neural concepts can be considered within the psychoanalytic space. Then, one can return to the neural space to consider what new possibilities exist for neuroscience when considering these novel relationships.

To continue with Blechner's (2018) example, drive (i.e., felt measure of demand) can be mapped by various neural circuits as in Panksepp's systems (first movement). However, in the psychoanalytic space (specifically, Blechner's mixed drive-relational space), these basic emotional systems *shape and are shaped by* relational formations, cognitive-affective interactions with the external world, especially with significant caregivers (second movement). Therefore, when returning to the neural space, one must consider the possibility of a brain which is itself relational.

With a relational understanding of Panksepp's systems, one can make a further step:

> When we consider multiple self-states . . . *the individual self-states may be affiliated with different drive-systems, thus connecting those self-states to different affects and different underlying patterns of brain structures, neurotransmitters, hormones, and other biological variables.*
>
> (Blechner, 2018, p. 676, emphases in the original)

This raises the question for neuroscience (third movement) of considering the brain not as a straightforwardly unitary organ (e.g., an individual's brain), but rather as a dynamic set of social systems (i.e., multiple self-states) that alter global brain functions based on current and prior relational configurations.

As I hope these examples illustrate, this threefold movement generates new *possibilities* for *both* disciplines. Such contributions are possible precisely via meta-neuropsychological bridges between objective and subjective lenses on the same *thing* (cf. dual-aspect monism). Dialogue generates possibilities and questions, not the certainty of knowledge, by reconfiguring the relationships among concepts. In this sense, neuropsychoanalysis is humble – it is up to *psychoanalysts* to explore the implications of neuroscience. The 'final court of appeals' for psychoanalysis remains the clinic (Solms, 2013).

Why Should Psychoanalysis Engage Neuroscience?

It is important to state clearly: no psychoanalyst *must* engage with neuroscience. Learning about the brain will not in itself make a good analyst. As noted on the 'clinical register' page of the International Neuropsychoanalysis Association website, which lists 'clinical fellows' who have undergone specialty training in neuropsychoanalysis:

> This Register is not meant to imply that all [neuropsychoanalysis society] members *should* undergo such training. One may be an excellent clinical practitioner without specialist training in neuropsychoanalysis.
> (npsa-association.org, 2021, emphasis in the original)

Importantly, the 'neuro-' prefix should be explicitly disconnected from any type of 'master discourse' (Bazan, 2020). As previously stated, neuroscience is not a field of superior knowledge. The following areas of contribution derive their advantage from the dialogic structure of neuropsychoanalysis, not any superior epistemology.

Research

Neuropsychoanalytic research is diverse, some of which remains close to analytic methods (e.g., analytical work with brain injury patients), while others explore psychoanalytic hypotheses using neuroscientific and psychological methods (i.e., psychodynamic neuroscience: questionnaires, brain imaging, social and cognitive experimental tasks, etc.). One might say that neuropsychoanalysis introduces new tools and concepts for generating and exploring psychoanalytic hypotheses (Salas and Palmer-Cancel, 2019). I will briefly illustrate how neuropsychoanalysis can contribute to one such question: *how does psychoanalysis effect clinical change?*

Moore et al. (2017) report a long-term (72 sessions, once per week) treatment of a patient who suffered an anoxic episode resulting in dense retrograde and anterograde amnesia. He was profoundly impaired in laying down new declarative, episodic memories. Episodic memories involve specific scenes and events which we can recall in our minds. This patient was thereby impaired in remembering therapy sessions. Despite minimal carry-over of explicit content between sessions, Moore et al. describe not only the generation of transferential feelings, but also the evolution of narcissistic dynamics (e.g., rejecting, taking in, etc.). They suggest that therapeutic change is not dependent upon declarative systems and that non-declarative procedural and emotional memories play an essential role. In terms of my threefold movement, one has selectively removed a piece of the neural space (focal lesion to medial temporal lobes impairing episodic memory) to observe dynamic changes to the remaining elements in the psychical sphere. The question arises of how the *talking cure* can affect *non-declarative* mental structures.

Bazan's (2011) Lacanian neuropsychoanalytic model of speech offers one possible roadmap by distinguishing between speech as a semantic, declarative process and speech as a motor articulatory (non-declarative) pattern. Specifically, the intention to execute a motor pattern generates (1) an outgoing motor command and (2) an 'efference copy.' The latter is the brain's prediction of the bodily state after the motor command has been executed. These signals typically balance out. When the motor command is inhibited, as often occurs with anxiety-linked traces, the efference copy remains unattenuated. Such residual tension operates at a higher conceptual level of motoric intentions. Freud's (1909) Rat Man case exemplifies the organizing role of abstract motor forms in mental life. For the Rat Man, *rat* acts as a formal pattern that links various scenes in the patient's life: marriage (*heiraten*), his childhood governess (Frau *Hofrat*), his monetary payment (*raten*) dilemma, and the (in)famous scene of anal torture by rats. Bazan proposes that interventions at the level of motor patterns, particularly those associated with emotional conflict and higher-order mental organization, are key to change.

Thus, in the case of Moore et al.'s patient, the process of speech as a motor pattern – rather than a semantic process – may have facilitated non-declarative structural change. One might argue that such a view places too strong an emphasis on language and symbolic thinking while neglecting the body. However, speech as a *non-declarative* motor form emphasizes language at the level of the non-declarative, procedural body.[3] It is the body, insofar as it *acts*, that enters speech.

This is but a single example of neurological analytic work and cognitive psychological research informing psychoanalytic hypotheses about clinical change. At this point, I would like to suggest a system of neuropsychoanalytic research which extends the case study method mentioned previously. Many quantitative and qualitative methods exist in psychotherapy research, such as thematic coding (Luborsky and Crits-Christoph, 1998), word-use (Pennebaker et al., 2015), discourse analysis (Hook, 2013), and so on. By collecting transcripts of psychotherapy with neurologic patients, one can extract qualitatively rich data to compare groups with different brain injuries. Quantitative coding of the same narrative data can facilitate large group comparisons, connections to standard (neuro)psychological assessments, and more confident conclusions than single cases alone. Regarding Moore et al.'s case, one might analyze how non-declarative dimensions of speech – syntax, word use (e.g., pronouns, negations), phonetic/phonemic elements, prosody, rhythm, and so on – change over time (and following therapeutic interventions) and how such changes relate to the overt (declarative) topics discussed.

In keeping with dual-aspect monism, no neuropsychoanalytic research is itself fit to 'prove' or 'disprove' psychoanalytic theory. This is not to say that empirical implications of psychoanalysis should not be subject to empirical testing. Rather, research and practice must maintain a balanced dialogue between study findings and clinical work.

The Social Situation of Psychoanalysis

Some might object that putting psychoanalysis into neuroscientific terms for research dilutes its concepts, uprooting them from their clinical context. This is why the neurologic patient method is considered the foundational neuropsychoanalytic methodology (Kaplan-Solms and Solms,

2002). Nevertheless, using neuroscientific terminology can be helpful, especially in the current socio-political milieu of psychoanalysis.

Moreover, in a clinical context, the analyst does not impose psychoanalytic terms onto the analysand. Rather, the analyst uses the analysand's own language and makes analytic interventions *in the patient's terms*. Analogously, neuropsychoanalysis allows psychoanalytic interventions *in neuroscientific terms*. Brain science dominates the mental health fields today. Using neuroscientific concepts and terminology (oriented by psychoanalytic meta-psychology; cf. threefold movement) allows psychoanalysis to immanently engage with neuroscience and psychology more broadly.

For example, the randomized clinical trial (RCT) model (where patients are randomly assigned to two different treatments and compared at outcome, to compare the effectiveness of each treatment) is the gold-standard for psychotherapy outcome research. However, it is not without its limitations relative to the naturalistic and messy clinical reality (Shedler, 2010). Rather than reject the RCT paradigm, however, one should intervene *within* it.

Marianne Leuzinger-Bohleber's psychoanalytic outcome project (the LAC study) in chronically depressed patients is exemplary (Leuzinger-Bohleber et al., 2019). While many studies have established the efficacy of short-term psychodynamic therapy (Shedler, 2010), Leuzinger-Bohleber et al.'s study seeks to (1) assess *long-term* (e.g., multi-year) psychoanalytic treatment in (2) the *naturalistic* context of patient choice. Patients were assessed in the context of seeing therapists with the choice of either cognitive-behavioral therapy (CBT) or psychoanalytic therapy (PAT). Outcome measures involved traditional depression symptom self-report questionnaires alongside a psychoanalytic measure of 'structural change.' This involved videorecorded, semi-structured interviews, which were assessed by trained (and blind) psychoanalytic coders along five axes:

Axis I: Experience of illness and prerequisites for treatment.
Axis II: Interpersonal relations (transference and countertransference).
Axis III: Life-defining and unconscious conflicts of the patient.
Axis IV: Structure (i.e., basal features of mental functioning).
Axis V: Mental and psychosomatic disorders in accordance with the established descriptive phenomenological diagnostics (ICD-10) (Leuzinger-Bohleber et al., 2019, p. 107).

Current analyses have found substantial improvements in depressive symptoms (by self-report) between years 1 and 3, indicating the efficacy of both treatments. Yet, there were no differences between CBT and PAT groups by self-reported symptoms at either timepoint. This hearkens to the infamous dodo bird verdict of psychotherapy (Shedler, 2010): all are equal (and therefore, choose the cheaper and faster therapy).

Psychoanalysts have emphasized that analysis leads not only to symptom reduction but to deep (and more meaningful) structural change. Accordingly, regarding axes III and IV in the LAC study, the PAT group showed significantly greater structural change (~60 percent, compared to ~36 percent in the CBT group) at year 3. Moreover, structural change in the PAT group only was associated with lower depression self-report scores (Leuzinger-Bohleber et al., 2019).

The LAC study is a 'case-in-point' of psychoanalysis engaging with (rather than externally critiquing) the language and methodologies of contemporary brain sciences (e.g., RCT). One can not only attend to psychoanalytic concepts (e.g., structural change) *within* an RCT paradigm but also demonstrate its relevance to traditional 'gold-standard' measures (i.e., the relationship between structural change and symptom change). Pre- versus post-treatment brain imaging comparisons (as planned in the follow-up study; Leuzinger-Bohleber, 2020) can further explore how changes in neuro-dynamic activity patterns relate to structure and symptoms. This is not to reduce psychoanalysis to RCT, but to demonstrate its capacity to critically engage within the field.

In addition, such engagement can broaden the academic milieu of psychoanalysis. Psychoanalysis is increasingly absent from graduate-level psychology programs, at least in the United States (Levy and Anderson, 2013). At the undergraduate level, psychoanalysis is less present in STEM and mainly found in the humanities. This climate exacerbates psychoanalytic isolationism, with corresponding negative effects at the socio-political level of insurance, funding, and accessibility (Leuzinger-Bohleber et al., 2019). I do not suggest that psychoanalysis leave the humanities (which have been a rich cultivating space). Rather, neuropsychoanalysis presents an opportunity to bridge the STEM-humanities divide via the question of the mind (cf. same *thing* in nature). Such educational bridges might have broader repercussive effects by increasing familiarity, integrating psychoanalytic ideas into research trends, and so on (Yovell et al., 2015).

While psychoanalysis should not bow to (and is often structurally opposed to) hegemonic social demands (e.g., funding, insurance, etc.), pragmatism is equally important. Neuropsychoanalysis can broaden the receptive field of psychoanalysis in academia to those who are less likely to be exposed to psychoanalysis (e.g., in the sciences) or those who may find the theoretical concepts too distant. Psychoanalysis can make a significant academic impact, which will be heard by more ears if it engages with the language of cognitive psychology and neuroscience. Such bottom-up exposure might cultivate sustained social changes, which have very real effects on practice.

Practice: Treating an Embodied Psyche

There is ongoing debate over how neuroscience impacts clinical practice (Fisher, 2020). It is important to point out that 'neuroscience impacting analytic practice' does not necessarily entail a bio-reductionistic approach. Any analyst, regardless of orientation, holds some meta-psychological framework in mind, informing *how* they approach clinical work (Sandberg, 2019). As Fisher puts it:

> By sharpening theoretical constructions, as background knowledge in the mind of the analyst, interdisciplinary study primes the psychoanalyst's observations about the patient, the analyst's self, and the dyad.
>
> (Fisher, 2020, p. 5)

An analyst should know how to 'use theory without believing in it' (Azeen Khan, personal communication). That is, one must be informed by theory while also being open to the idiosyncrasy of the clinical encounter. The issue of bio- (or any) reductionism is therefore not unique to neuropsychoanalysis.

Attention to the body is one salient topic 'primed' by neuroscientific knowledge. In dialogue with computational neuroscience and predictive coding, Solms (2018) offers a broad-brushstroke overview of his clinical method. For him, the subject is faced with unmet needs – especially Panksepp's drives – that generate affect when deviated from their set-points. Affect is registered as *prediction error*.[4] Errors signal a deviation from where the organism 'should be' and motivate the work to return to the desired state. The subject must form a predictive model (an inferred representation) of its body and the world to monitor and meet its needs. This entails updating *predictions*, which take two broad states: perception (updating the representational model) and action (acting in the world to meet the model). Importantly, prediction may be declarative (e.g., episodic memory, working memory) or non-declarative (e.g., procedural/emotional action plans).

For Solms (2018), the essence of psychopathology is 'prematurely automatized predictions,' habituated predictions which *do not work*. In childhood, the little subject with limited cognitive capacities is faced with myriad needs that cannot all be satisfied in its complex relational world. Thus, the little subject makes 'the best of a bad job' and automatizes predictions which *do not* satisfy the emotional needs, leaving some affect (prediction error) left over. Since these faulty predictions are automatized, they repeat throughout life, generating ongoing prediction error. Thus, patients suffer from feelings. It is a problem of deeply learned predictive patterns that fail to meet the demands of the drives.

Substantial research in memory reconsolidation suggests that the arousal of prediction error renders the associated memory (prediction) labile. Solms suggests that psychoanalysis works by *problematizing* (linking predictions to their felt errors) inadequate ways of meeting one's needs, rendering such predictions labile. This opens the space for working-through and laying down *new*, better ways of meeting emotional needs.

As Solms (2018) points out, prematurely automatized predictions *cannot* be reconsolidated in declarative thought because they are procedural (non-declarative) in nature. They can only be reconsolidated through *embodied enactments*. This returns us to the question of the non-declarative body.

Discussing a special issue of *Psychoanalytic Inquiry* (volume 39, issue 8) on the impact of neuroscience on psychoanalysts, Sandberg (2019) notes that one common focus for the authors was how neuroscience informs thinking about the body, especially the primacy of somatic-affective experience. Whether discussing bodily references in language, symbolizing bodily experiences, or bodily enactments, these authors illustrate how neuropsychoanalysis attunes the analyst to bodily issues as they unfold in the analytic duo. I would add here a reference to Bazan's (2011) Lacanian point of the motoric aspect of speech – the *speaking body* – as the nodal point of the talking cure and the embodied psyche.

Interestingly, two authors in the above mentioned special issue use Antonio Damasio's framework, yet come to different conclusions (Sandberg, 2019). Lombardi (2019) emphasizes that the body is the 'first object to be known' and posits a primordial relationship to the body. Sletvold (2019), in contrast, emphasizes that core bodily representations are already in (non-egoic) interface with the interpersonal world – emphasizing that the body is primarily interpersonal. Such interpretations illustrate how neuroscientific dialogue non-deterministically opens space to rethink differences between analytic approaches.[5]

Moreover, today, the fact of our embodiment is increasingly exploited, whether through technology or psychotropic medications. For example, of the 19.2% of adults in the United States who received mental health treatment in 2019, 15.8% took medications. That is, 82.29% of adult patients receiving mental health treatment received medications (Terlizzi and Zablotsky, 2020). It is insufficient for psychoanalysis to only consider how patients make sense of their experience of medication. While meaning is essential, the fact remains that psychotropics not only *directly* impact brain chemistry – different drugs differentially impact the major drive systems which exert considerable influence over cognitive processes (Panksepp, 1998). For example, stimulants (dopamine agonists) act primarily on SEEKING whereas opiates act primarily on PANIC.

Knowledge of how emotional systems are affected by different medications can inform how an analyst might understand transference-countertransference (Johnson and Mosri, 2016) or dimensions of satisfaction (Dall'Aglio, 2020) with these patients. A patient on opiates might experience less desire for social connectedness because this need (PANIC) is being medicated (Johnson and Mosri, 2016). This is not to index every attachment-related issue (or lack thereof) to the medication – such knowledge participates as one factor among many in the analytic exploration (cf. threefold movement).

Building Bridges

As psychoanalysis has evolved, different schools have developed their own meta-psychologies and clinical approaches. Because of each school's complexity, expertise in multiple schools has become increasingly difficult, leading to a 'tower of Babel' issue (Karbelnig, 2018). Today, the term 'drive' can mean something very different to two analysts.

Neuropsychoanalysis has the unique potential to bridge different analytic schools. One can map the brain from different meta-psychological perspectives (e.g., Dall'Aglio, 2019; Lombardi, 2019; Sletvold, 2019; Solms, 2013) or work with neurologic patients from different orientations (e.g., Morin, 2018; Salas et al., 2021). The previous discussion of classical drives and relational needs is one example. By approaching the brain from different perspectives – where the same area might be discussed in terms 'X' from one approach and in terms 'Y' from another – one can suppose a theoretically and clinically meaningful connection between terms X and Y. This is a convergence, in neural space, of concepts that belong to distinct analytic schools (cf. threefold movement). I do not suggest a unification of analytic schools. Rather, I believe that the brain can be a 'meeting-ground' to sharpen theoretical differences and explore key questions in new light.

Moreover, neuropsychoanalytic dialogue can function as a broader bridge between sciences and humanities because of the dual approaches to the same *thing-in-nature*. For example, Solms's (2021) work on the philosophical hard problem of consciousness (how subjectivity arises from brain physiology) has highlighted affect as the fundamental stuff of consciousness (more on this later). Issues arising from the focus on cognitive (e.g., visual) consciousness (namely, that all cognitive processes can function *without* subjective experience, the 'something-it-is-like'-ness of being) disappear when placing affect front and center. There is *necessarily* 'something-it-is-like' to feel a feeling. Likewise, work addressing the relationship between the constitutive parts of the *thing-in-nature* (e.g., quantum physics, brain-machine interface) and the productions of that *thing* (e.g., political issues, ethics, culture) can benefit from a dialogue which pivots on the subjective and objective perspectives of that same *thing-in-nature*.

Shifting Paradigms

Perhaps most significant about neuropsychoanalytic dialogue is the potential for fundamental paradigm shifts. To use another analogy from Freudian theory, just as knowledge of repressed material does not undo repression (Freud, 1925a), the addition of knowledge (e.g., from neuroscience to psychoanalysis) alone does not shift the fundamental coordinates of a discipline. Reworking the *relationships between concepts* – above the addition of concepts – can reorient the fault-lines upon which neuroscience and psychoanalysis describe the basic challenges of subjective life.

A remarkable paradigm shift for psychoanalysis is Solms's (2013) thesis of the 'conscious id.' Reviewing a range of neuropsychological literature, Solms describes how the brain areas associated with internal bodily regulation and somatic-affective demands (i.e., the brainstem and associated limbic structures) are functionally correlative with Freud's id. The neocortex, on the other hand, with its representational and cognitive faculties, is functionally correlated to the ego. Solms highlights that damage to neocortical regions alters the *quality* of consciousness but does not remove sentience. In contrast, damage to key brainstem areas completely *wipes out* consciousness. The brainstem appears to be necessary for consciousness, with neocortical cognitive consciousness dependent upon brainstem arousal. Therefore, Solms proposes, the id (i.e., the brainstem) must be conscious.

The ongoing debate regarding this 'conscious id' (cf. Hartmann Cardelle, 2019) indicates how Solms's thesis is 'sufficiently radical that [it] require[s] substantial work to integrate with psychoanalytic theory' (Fisher, 2020, p. 3). In my view, its most profound claim is that the id is *affectively conscious*. That is, consciousness is fundamentally a non-representational (i.e., non-cognitive) arousal. This introduces *levels* of consciousness, where affective consciousness must be distinguished from cognitive consciousness (Dall'Aglio, 2021b). Recall that Freud (1923) had linked consciousness with perception (i.e., cognition). The division of consciousness – and affective (non-representational, non-reflexive) consciousness in particular – is a radically new notion for psychoanalysis.

Solms's conscious id thereby reconfigures the basic tension in Freudian theory. While the conscious-unconscious split remains essential (cf. premature automatization), affective consciousness (i.e., felt uncertainty in relation to drive-demand) is the motor force. Freud (1925b) placed his insight of the unconscious among the great 'narcissistic insults to man' (alongside Copernicus and Darwin). I suggest that Solms, read in this light, makes a similar blow. Not only does the unconscious hold sway over the ego – *consciousness itself is no longer (fundamentally) egoic*. The root of our subjective experience is radically exterior to our 'I' (Dall'Aglio, 2021a, b). Linking the *cognitive ego* with the *feeling subject* of affective consciousness might therefore be a socio-cognitive achievement, not an elementary given. Cases of trauma or brain injury (e.g., Zúñiga, 2017) amply demonstrate how insults to our cognitive (egoic) capacities unmask the exteriority of our affective core. In the neural space, one has found a convergence of consciousness and non-representational affect (cf. three-fold movement) – the implications regarding consciousness for psychoanalysis are paradigm-shifting.

Toward a Neuropsychoanalytic Materialism

I began this chapter by asking *what sort of (neuro)science could include psychoanalysis?* and *what sort of psychoanalysis could include neuroscience?* My discussion pivoted on an open dialogue where novel ideas or relationships from one discipline inspire possibilities in the other. In a certain sense, I am advocating for epistemological openness. But interdisciplinary openness is (ideally) an aspect of *any* discipline. A more precise answer to these questions requires an explicit thinking of the relationship of each discipline (i.e., epistemology) to the *thing-in-nature* (i.e., ontology).

Here, I rely heavily on the philosophical framework of 'Transcendental Materialism' developed by Adrian Johnston (2019). I am also detailing more explicitly the position I have taken elsewhere (Dall'Aglio, 2019, 2020, 2021a) regarding Lacanian neuropsychoanalysis. A full discussion is beyond the scope of this chapter, so I will focus on addressing these two *what sort of . . .* questions. Whereas my previous comments primarily relied on points of *connection* and conceptual 'bilingualism,' this (re)thinking will focus more on points of *disjuncture* within and between disciplines.

Recall that dual-aspect monism posits two unique but incomplete perspectives on the *thing-in-nature*. Neuroscience and psychoanalysis are limited, unable to fully grasp it. A gap exists between epistemology and ontology, in addition to the phenomenological-epistemic gap between epistemologies (Figure 6.1). These are two aspects of the 'frontier-discipline' nature of neuropsychoanalysis, straddling the subjective-objective limitation.

Importantly, such a 'mind-body' tension exists within psychoanalysis with 'drive as a concept on the frontier between the mental and the somatic' (Freud, 1915, pp. 121–122). Likewise, the neurosciences produce a split within the brain, where representations of the internal milieu are of a completely different quality – namely, somatic-affective – from representations of the external world of cognitive objects (Solms,

2013). An incommensurability is *(re)produced within* each epistemology: between cognitive-affective in neuroscience, and between drive-demand and representational work in psychoanalysis (more discussion of such antagonisms later).

These antagonisms should be taken seriously. As suggested by Žižek (2020), conceptual limitations should not be viewed as epistemological deficits. Rather, true conflicts or paradoxes indicate something about the *thing*, a certain *antagonism-in-nature*. Instead of asking how to resolve such limits, this view shifts to another question: *what must the 'nature of human nature' be* to produce such disparate epistemological lenses?

Transcendental Materialism: A Weak Nature Alone

The notion of *antagonism-in-nature* is central to Johnston's transcendental materialism. Simply put, Johnston proposes a materialistic view of nature that rejects any super-natural dimension unique to humans. Nevertheless, this same nature gives rise to a distinctly human dimension which is irreducible to 'natural laws.' This is because 'natural laws' are not all-determining, in the sense of a 'Nature' fully explained by a set of rules. Rather than a unified, harmonious Nature often stereotyped in mainstream culture (e.g., the conventional *National Geographic* documentary), John-ston emphasizes nature – especially the increased complexity of organic life – as an ongoing series of accidents, conflicts, and rifts.

For example, evolution is not a teleological process *aiming* toward a higher intelligent design. It is essentially a series of catastrophes. Evolution progresses when something is going *existentially wrong* for a species. Such progress is *accidental*, based on genetic mutations and epigenetic circum-stances. Common parlance speaks of 'X evolved to do Y,' when it is per-haps more accurate to say 'X evolved and just so happened to deal with Y.'

Johnston calls this image of nature a 'weak nature alone.' The evolution-ary low bar of 'survive and reproduce' leaves ample room for non-fatal, self-sabotaging short-circuits. Living organisms are especially prone to such disjunctures – increased complexity coincides with rifts between disorgan-ized evolutionary systems haplessly clumped together. Importantly, these *antagonisms-in-nature* have a causal role of their own (more on this later).

A few illustrative examples indicate how the brain is perhaps the peak of nature's complexity. Extracting arguments from David Linden and Anto-nio Damasio, Johnston highlights the brain as a 'kludge' of evolutionary disjoint systems, in no way consonant with each other, sedimented over phylogeny (with evolutionarily older systems preserved alongside recently evolved ones). The split between ancient somatic-affective brainstem regions and recent neocortical cognitive processes is but one example. Their agendas differ significantly (i.e., context-sensitive neocortex versus the brainstem's generalized, high-priority affective demands), but they are 'forced to cooperate' in the quest for homeostasis.

Regarding the neural correlates of consciousness, Feinberg (2012) highlights how the increasing complexity of neural hierarchies entails an inability of higher levels (e.g., cognitive work) to access earlier processing stages (e.g., somatic-affective registration). This is a possible correlate of the irreconcilability between subjective first-person and objective third-person perspectives. Feinberg hypothesizes that this irreconcilability is one of the conditions for conscious qualia.

Moreover, the brain's multiple emotional needs inevitably conflict, in the complexity of interpersonal situations and the fact that some systems are at odds with each other (e.g., SEEKING increased excitation versus PANIC-motivated security). They are *categorically* distinct, with no genetic algorithm for which need to prioritize in which context. Paradoxically, this 'built-in' conflict (and non-resolution of drive-tension) is a prerequisite for affective consciousness (Solms, 2021). This affective bedrock is the subject's feeling its way through the uncertainty arising from evolutionary complexity and unpredictable present circumstances. In sum, various authors have highlighted a certain antagonism within the brain as having an important role regarding how the brain relates to human subjectivity.

Transcendental Materialism and Dual-Aspect Monism

With regard to neuropsychoanalytic dual-aspect monism, transcendental materialism emphasizes antagonism (on both neural and psychological sides) and places 'weak nature' at the ontological *thing-in-nature*, an *antagonism-in-nature* (see Figure 6.2). In terms of my threefold movement, the antagonism within and between epistemologies is itself a concept to consider at the level of ontology. *Antagonism-in-nature* – out-of-joint complex material substrates – immanently produces radically different (subjective, objective) epistemological lenses that turnabout and perceive that same substrate from two very different perspectives.

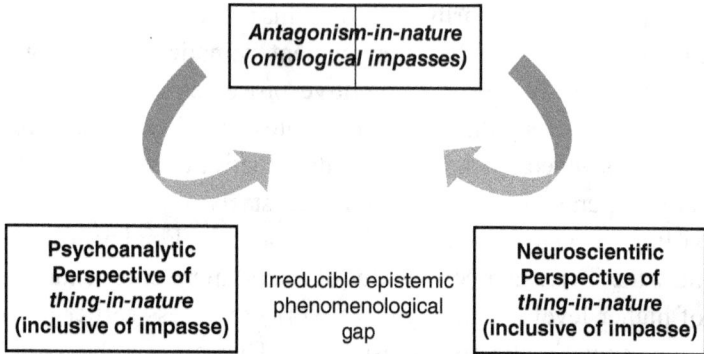

Figure 6.2 Visual depiction of dual-aspect monism (see Figure 6.1) supplemented by transcendental materialism. The *antagonism-in-nature* emphasizes how epistemic antagonisms are not only due to limitations of perspective but are (in some cases) touching upon ontological rifts. The reflexive arrows indicate how observational perspectives are not independent of the *thing-in-nature* — they arise from and are part of nature.

One important implication of this position is that neuropsychoanalytic meta-psychology should not only be built upon functional correlations. Failures, limitations, complexities, and contradictions should also be sought as bridge-sites. These tensions indicate key features of *antagonism-in-nature* and indicate how limitations in one framework open upon the space of the other.

In anticipation of a criticism that transcendental materialism is an irrelevant philosophical exercise, I (re)emphasize that *antagonism-in-nature* has its consequences. Complexity between competing needs preserves the uncertain space of affective consciousness, which is the basis of all consciousness (Solms, 2021). To give another example, Bazan and Detandt (2013) highlight the difference between internal bodily processes (oriented toward visceral needs) and external bodily processes associated with muscular actions. There is an antagonism between these 'two bodies' (Dall'Aglio, 2021a) – the muscular body has no a priori knowledge of which actions satisfy which internal needs. Another brain system – the mesolimbic dopaminergic SEEKING system – fills the gap left by this lack of internal-external rapport. Dopamine spikes record the surprising satisfaction of internal needs by specific motor actions. Such dynamics historicize the individual's *linking* of need with action.

Importantly, the actions 'tagged' by dopamine bursts generate a rewarding quality of their own, such that the repetition of those actions brings its own enjoyment distinct from the satisfaction of internal needs (this is the neurochemical side of addictive processes). Bazan (2011) emphasizes that this motoric dimension is the wellspring of uniquely mental life. Indeed, some of our most complex cognitive functions are extensions of this motoric system and rely on dopamine spikes for learning. Importantly, this space is generated by an irreducible limit between internal needs and the brain systems tasked with meeting them. That such systems can be exploited (for example, social media algorithms were *intentionally* designed upon the addictive dynamics of this system; Orlowski, 2020) draws attention to human nature not as a space of natural balance but as a complex, conflicting space prone to denaturalization.

Reprise: What Sort of (Neuro)science? What Sort of Psychoanalysis?

One of the primary issues with the question *what sort of (neuro)science could include psychoanalysis?* is that science is often envisioned as reducing the mind to the brain as a part of nature, a unified world of determinate laws. However, with an image of nature given by transcendental materialism, I propose that it is precisely a science of *weak nature* that could include psychoanalysis, insofar as the human dimension arises from the material yet is irreducible to explanation at the level of that substrate. Or rather, it is reducible to that material substrate *at the point where that substrate encounters a conflict within itself.*

Likewise, the question of *what sort of psychoanalysis could include science?* requires a psychoanalysis which places the mind among other things in nature – thus relinquishing various trends toward mental or symbolic reductionism. An ontology of weak nature creates this space *within nature* without a resort to any a priori (and therefore unexplained) dimension beyond the natural world. The gap traditionally situated between the mental and the material should be transcribed into an *antagonism* of the material, the hodgepodge complexity of disjointed natural processes which paradoxically give rise to the uniquely human dimensions that psychoanalysis concerns itself with.

For neuropsychoanalysis to be an answer to *what sort of psychoanalysis . . .* and *what sort of (neuro)science . . .* I suggest that neuropsychoanalysis consider what might come of situating its philosophical basis along the lines of transcendental materialism (Figure 6.2). Specifically, I pose the following questions:

- Does a *weak nature* ontology change epistemological conceptions of the mind or brain in psychoanalysis and neuroscience?
- Does transcendental materialism give neuropsychoanalysis a new framework to address the epistemological challenges of bridging objective and subjective lenses?[6]
- What research or clinical implications arise from the framework of transcendental materialism? Are they unique to transcendental materialism?

As with the dialogic basis of neuropsychoanalysis, I put forward these questions in a genuine spirit of open exploration. I believe it is through dialogue that new avenues emerge and paradigm shifting ideas arise.

To Conclude: Exploring the Frontier

There is a plurality of viewpoints within neuropsychoanalysis. In this chapter, I have presented some of my own and attempted to situate certain areas of neuropsychoanalytic work in a dialogic structure. I encourage the curious reader to confer with publications in the *Neuropsychoanalysis* journal, *Frontiers in Psychology | Psychoanalysis and Neuropsychoanalysis*, and elsewhere (e.g., *Psychoanalytic Inquiry* special issue 39:8) to explore the diversity of theoretical viewpoints, research, and clinical applications that have generated such rich ongoing discussions. Neuropsychoanalysis is truly a 'land of unlimited opportunities' (to paraphrase Freud, 1920). Equipped with an equal footing of objective and subjective paradigms, we can take our steps and feel our way through the uncertainty at the frontiers of the 'minded brain.'

Notes

1 My views blend 'Anglo-American' and 'Lacanian' neuropsychoanalysis. Given the diversity of viewpoints in neuropsychoanalysis, some may disagree with me on certain points. These are welcome disagreements – they point to sites for future discussion and research.
2 Capitalization follows Panksepp's call for a unique lexicon for speaking of these systems, to distinguish them from descriptive words.
3 I am here extending a position first elaborated elsewhere (Dall'Aglio, 2021a).

4 I am leaving precision out of this discussion for simplicity. Affect is a specifically prioritized prediction error.
5 Similarly, there are different interpretations of data by neuroscientists. For
example, regarding affect, Panksepp (1998) argues for subcortical emotional
systems, whereas LeDoux (LeDoux and Brown, 2017) emphasizes cortical processing. These different neuroscientific theories lead to different neuropsychoanalytic views of emotion (Bazan, 2020; Solms, 2021). See Dall'Aglio (2021a)
for a neuropsychoanalytic reconsideration of this difference.
6 This is the topic of a paper in preparation.

References

Bazan, A. (2011). Phantoms in the voice: A neuropsychoanalytic hypothesis
on the structure of the unconscious. *Neuropsychoanalysis*, 13(2), 161–176.
doi:10.1080/15294145.2011.10773672.

Bazan, A. (2020). Elaborating a science of the mental. *Neuropsychoanalysis*,
21(2), 92–95. doi:10.1080/15294145.2019.1695978.

Bazan, A. & Detandt, S. (2013). On the physiology of jouissance: Interpreting the
mesolimbic dopaminergic reward functions from a psychoanalytic perspective.
Frontiers in Human Neuroscience, 7(709). doi:10.3389/fnhum.2013.00709.

———. (2015). Trauma and jouissance: A neuropsychoanalytic perspective.
Journal of the Centre for Freudian Analysis and Research, 26, 99–127.

Blass, R. & Carmeli, Z. (2007). The case against neuropsychoanalysis: On fallacies underlying psychoanalysis' latest scientific trend and its negative impact
on psychoanalytic discourse. *International Journal of Psychoanalysis*, 88(1),
19–40. doi:10.1516/6NCA-A4MA-MFQ7-0JTJ.

Blechner, M. (2018). Data, dreams, and drives: Interpersonal and relational inno-
vations in perspective. *Psychoanalytic Dialogues*, 28(6), 670–678. doi:10.1080/
10481885.2018.1538744.

Dall'Aglio, J. (2019). Of brains and Borromean knots: A Lacanian meta-
neuropsychology. *Neuropsychoanalysis*, 21(1), 23–38. doi:10.1080/15294145.
2019.1619091.

———. (2020). No-Thing in common between the unconscious and the brain: On
the (im)possibility of Lacanian neuropsychoanalysis. *Psychoanalysis Lacan*, 4.
Retrieved from http://psychoanalysislacan.com/issue-4/.

———. (2021a). Sex and prediction error part two: Jouissance and the free
energy principle in neuropsychoanalysis. *Journal of the American Psychoanalytic Association*, 69(4), 715–741. doi:10.1177/00030651211042377.

———. (2021b). What can psychoanalysis learn from neuroscience? A theoretical basis for the emergence of a neuropsychoanalytic model. *Contemporary
Psychoanalysis*, 57(1), 125–145. doi:10.1080/00107530.2021.1894542.

Feinberg, T. (2012). Neuroontology, neurobiological naturalism, and consciousness: A challenge to scientific reduction and a solution. *Physics of Life Reviews*,
9(1), 13–34. doi:10.1016/j.plrev.2011.10.019.

Fisher, C. (2020). Review of *Psychoanalytic Inquiry*, special issue 39:8 (2019). The influence of neuroscience on psychoanalysts: A contemporary perspective. *Neuropsychoanalysis*, 22(1–2), 151–160. doi:10.1080/15294145.2020.1852102.

Freud, S. (1895). Project for a scientific psychology. In Strachey, J. (ed. & Trans.), *The Standard Edition of the Complete Psychological Works of Sigmund Freud* (Vol. 1, pp. 281–391). London: Hogarth Press.

———. (1909). Notes upon a case of obsessional neurosis. In Strachey, J. (ed. & Trans.), *The Standard Edition of the Complete Psychological Works of Sigmund Freud* (Vol. 10, pp. 151–318). London: Hogarth Press.

———. (1915). Instincts and their vicissitudes. In Strachey, J. (ed. & Trans.), *The Standard Edition of the Complete Psychological Works of Sigmund Freud* (Vol. 14, pp. 109–140). London: Hogarth Press.

———. (1920). Beyond the pleasure principle. In Strachey, J. (ed. & Trans.), *The Standard Edition of the Complete Psychological Works of Sigmund Freud* (Vol. 18, pp. 1–64. London: Hogarth Press.

———. (1923). The ego and the id. In Strachey, J. (ed. & Trans.), *The Standard Edition of the Complete Psychological Works of Sigmund Freud* (Vol. 19, pp. 1–66). London: Hogarth Press.

———. (1925a). Negation. In Strachey, J. (ed. & Trans.), *The Standard Edition of the Complete Psychological Works of Sigmund Freud* (Vol. 19, pp. 233–240). London: Hogarth Press.

———. (1925b). The resistances to psycho-analysis. In Strachey, J. (ed. & Trans.), *The Standard Edition of the Complete Psychological Works of Sigmund Freud* (Vol. 19, pp. 211–224). London: Hogarth Press.

Greenberg, J. & Mitchell, S. (1983). *Object Relations in Psychoanalytic Theory*. Cambridge: Harvard University Press.

Hartmann Cardelle, V. (2019). Metapsychological consequences of the conscious brainstem: A critique of the conscious id. *Neuropsychoanalysis*, 21(1), 3–22. doi:10.1080/15294145.2019.1620628.

Hook, D. (2013). Tracking the Lacanian unconscious in language. *Psychodynamic Practice*, 19(1), 38–54. doi:10.1080/14753634.2013.750094.

Johnson, B. & Mosri, D. (2016). The neuropsychoanalytic approach: Using neuroscience as the basic science of psychoanalysis. *Frontiers in Psychology*, 7(1459). doi:10.3389/fpsyg.2016.01459.

Johnston, A. (2005). *Time Driven: Metapsychology and the Splitting of the Drive*. Evanston: Northwestern University Press.

———. (2019). *Prolegomena to Any Future Materialism, Volume Two: A Weak Nature Alone*. Evanston: Northwestern University Press.

Kaplan-Solms, K. & Solms, M. (2002). *Clinical Studies in Neuro-Psychoanalysis: Introduction to a Depth Neuropsychology*. Second edition. London: Karnac Books.

Karbelnig, A. (2018). Addressing psychoanalysis's post-tower of Babel linguistic challenge: A proposal for a cross-theoretical, clinical nomenclature. *Contemporary Psychoanalysis*, 54(2), 322–350.

Kessler, L. & Kessler, R. (2019). Neuropsychoanalytic explorations: Linking practice, theory, and research. *Psychoanalytic Inquiry*, 39(8), 582–595. doi:10.1080/07351690.2019.1671079.

Lacan, J. (1964). *The Seminar of Jacques Lacan: The Four Fundamental Concepts of Psychoanalysis* (J.-A. Miller, Ed., A. Sheridan, Trans.). New York: W. W. Norton & Company. 1978.

Laurent, É. (1995). Alienation and separation (I). In Feldstein, R., Fink, B. & Jaanus, M. (eds.), *Reading Seminar XI: Lacan's Four Fundamental Concepts of Psychoanalysis* (pp. 19–28). Albany: State University of New York Press.

LeDoux, J. & Brown, R. (2017). A higher-order theory of emotional consciousness. *PNAS* 114(1), E2016–E2025. doi:10.1073/pnas.1619316114.

Leuzinger-Bohleber, M. (2020). Bridging psychoanalysis and neuroscience in outcome studies: One example [Conference presentation]. *Neuropsychoanalysis Around the World* 2020, online meeting. Retrieved from https://npsa-association.org/education-training/videos1/webinar-videos/npsa-around-the-world-presentations-videos/.

Leuzinger-Bohleber, M., Kaufhold, J., Kallenbach, L., Negele, A., Ernst, M., Keller, W., Fiedler, G., Hautzinger, M., Bahrke, U. & Beutel, M. (2019). How to measure sustained psychic transformations in long-term treatments of chronically depressed patients: Symptomatic and structural changes in the LAC depression study of the outcome of cognitive-behavioural and psychoanalytic long-term treatments. *The International Journal of Psychoanalysis*, 100(1), 99–127. doi:10.1080/00207578.2018.1533377.

Levy, K. & Anderson, T. (2013). Is clinical psychology doctoral training becoming less intellectually diverse? And if so, what can be done? *Clinical Psychology: Science and Practice*, 20(2), 211–220. doi:10.1111/cpsp.12035.

Lombardi, R. (2019). Developing a capacity for bodily concern: Antonio Damasio and the psychoanalysis of body-mind relationship. *Psychoanalytic Inquiry*, 39(8), 534–544. doi:10.1080/07351690.2019.1671066.

Luborsky, L. & Crits-Christoph, P. (1998). *Understanding Transference: The Core Conflictual Relationship Theme Method*. Second edition. Washington, DC: American Psychological Association.

Moore, P., Salas, C., Dockree, S. & Turnbull, O. (2017). Observations on working psychoanalytically with a profoundly amnesic patient. *Frontiers in Psychology*, 8(1418). doi:10.3389/fpsyg.2017.01418.

Morin, C. (2018). *Stroke, Body Image, and Self-Representation: Psychoanalytic and Neurological Perspectives* (K. Valendinova & C. Morin, Trans.). New York: Routledge.

npsa-association.org. (2021, March 23). The clinical register of the International Neuropsychoanalysis Society. Retrieved from https://npsa-association.org/education-training/register-international-neuropsychoanalysis/.

Orlowski, J. (Director). (2020). *The Social Dilemma* [Motion picture].

Panksepp, J. (1998). *Affective Neuroscience: The Foundations of Human and Animal Emotions*. New York: Oxford University Press.

Pennebaker, J. W., Booth, R. J., Boyd, R. L. & Francis, M. E. (2015). *Linguistic Inquiry and Word Count: LIWC2015*. Austin, TX: Pennebaker Conglomerates. Retrieved from www.LIWC.net.

Salas, C. & Palmer-Cancel, S. (2019). Neuropsychoanalytic 20 years later: An interview with Oliver Turnbull. *Neuropsychoanalysis*, 21(1), 39–45. doi:10.10 80/15294145.2019.1631039.

Salas, C., Turnbull, O. & Solms, M. (2021). *Clinical Studies in Neuropsychoanalysis Revisited*. London and New York: Routledge.

Sandberg, L. (2019). Interpreting neuroscientific facts. *Psychoanalytic Inquiry*, 39(8), 596–606. doi:10.1080/07351690.2019.1671124.

Shedler, J. (2010). The efficacy of psychodynamic psychotherapy. *American Psychologist*, 65(2), 98–109. doi:10.1037/a0018378.

Sletvold, J. (2019). Neuroscience and the embodiment of psychoanalysis – With an appreciation of Damasio's contribution. *Psychoanalytic Inquiry*, 39(8), 545–556. doi:10.1080/07351690.2019.1671067.

Solms, M. (2013). The conscious id. *Neuropsychoanalysis*, 15(1), 5–19. doi:10.1080/15294145.2013.10773711.

———. (2015). *The Feeling Brain. Selected Papers on Neuropsychoanalysis*. London: Karnac Books.

———. (2018). The neurobiological underpinnings of psychoanalytic theory and therapy. *Frontiers in Behavioral Neuroscience*, 12(294). doi:10.3389/fnbeh.2018.00294.

———. (2021). *The Hidden Spring: A Journey to the Source of Consciousness*. London: Profile Books.

Terlizzi, E. & Zablotsky, B. (2020). *Mental Health Treatment Among Adults: United States, 2019. NCHS Data Brief, 380*. Hyattsville, MD: National Center for Health Statistics.

Yovell, Y., Solms, M. & Fotopoulou, A. (2015). The case for neuropsychoanalysis: Why a dialogue with neuroscience is necessary but not sufficient for psychoanalysis. *The International Journal of Psychoanalysis*, 96(6), 1515–1553. doi:10.1111/1745-8315.12332.

Žižek, S. (2020). *Sex and the Failed Absolute*. London: Bloomsbury.

Zúñiga, J. F. M. (2017). EnRAGEd: Introductory notes on aggression in a case of orbitofrontal syndrome. *Neuropsychoanalysis*, 19(1), 77–86. doi:10.1080/1529 4145.2017.1295816.

Index

For Product Safety Concerns and Information please contact our EU
representative GPSR@taylorandfrancis.com
Taylor & Francis Verlag GmbH, Kaufingerstraße 24, 80331 München, Germany

* 9 7 8 1 0 3 2 2 2 1 9 2 2 *